FORGING EUROPE'S LEADERSHIP

The Foundation for European Progressive Studies (FEPS) is the think tank of the progressive political family at EU level. Our mission is to develop innovative research, policy advice, training and debates to inspire and inform progressive politics and policies across Europe. We operate as hub for thinking to facilitate the emergence of progressive answers to the challenges that Europe faces today.

FEPS works in close partnership with its members and partners, forging connections and boosting coherence among stakeholders from the world of politics, academia and civil society at local, regional, national, European and global levels.

Today FEPS benefits from a solid network of 68 member organisations. Among these, 43 are full members, 20 have observer status and 5 are ex-officio members. In addition to this network of organisations that are active in the promotion of progressive values, FEPS also has an extensive network of partners, including renowned universities, scholars, policymakers and activists.

Our ambition is to undertake intellectual reflection for the benefit of the progressive movement, and to promote the founding principles of the EU – freedom, equality, solidarity, democracy, respect of human rights, fundamental freedoms and human dignity, and respect of the rule of law.

This book has been published in cooperation with:

Karl Renner Institut
Karl-Popper-Straße 8,
A-1100 Vienna, Austria
www.renner-institut.at

Olof Palme International Center
Sveavägen 68,
111 34 Stockholm, Sweden
www.palmecenter.se

Fondation Jean-Jaurès
12 Cité Malesherbes,
75009 Paris, France
www.jean-jaures.org

FORGING EUROPE'S LEADERSHIP
GLOBAL TRENDS, RUSSIAN AGGRESSION AND THE RISK OF A REGRESSIVE WORLD

Edited by Giovanni Grevi

Copyright © 2023 Foundation for European Progressive Studies

Book published in September 2023 by the Foundation for European Progressive Studies in association with London Publishing Partnership

FOUNDATION FOR EUROPEAN PROGRESSIVE STUDIES (FEPS)
Avenue des Arts 46 – 1000 Brussels, Belgium
www.feps-europe.eu
@FEPS_Europe

Supervision: Hedwig Giusto
Project coordination: David Rinaldi, Andriy Korniychuk, Thainá Leite and Giovanni Grevi
Layout and editing: T&T Productions Ltd, London

This book was published with the financial support of the European Parliament. It does not represent the view of the European Parliament.

A catalogue record for this book is available from the British Library

ISBN: 978-1-913019-97-6 (pbk)
ISBN: 978-1-913019-98-3 (ePDF)
ISBN: 978-1-913019-99-0 (ePUB)

Table of contents

Giovanni Grevi
Introduction   1

Andriy Korniychuk
1 | Geopolitical crossroads: the strategic landscape after Russia's invasion of Ukraine   7

Thijs Van de Graaf
2 | The geopolitics of energy after Russia's war in Ukraine   25

Thomas Pellerin-Carlin
3 | Overcoming the great fossil fuel shock: building an energy system that serves a free, secure and green Europe   41

George Papaconstantinou
4 | The global economic disorder: drifting towards fragmentation   52

Elvire Fabry
5 | Global trade and investment: the rising economic security paradigm   68

Annalisa Prizzon
6 | A growing gap between development cooperation and development needs   81

Daniela Schwarzer
7 | The EU put to the test: fast forward, catching up or lagging behind?   **92**

Giovanni Grevi
Conclusion: averting a regressive world – global trends and Europe's leadership   **107**

About the authors   **135**

Giovanni Grevi

Introduction

This book is the final product of a major foresight project launched by the Foundation for European Progressive Studies in mid-2022 to explore the long-term implications of the war in Ukraine. Russia's aggression against Ukraine marked a historic turning point, upending earlier assumptions, carrying wide-ranging ramifications and fuelling uncertainty on the global stage. If the fog of war clouds prospects on the outcome of the conflict, it is certain that the implications of Russia's aggression will unfold over many years and affect the shape of the international order. The question is how.

Since February 2022 the imperative to support Ukraine, push Russia back and cope with the threats that Russia's attack poses to regional and global stability has inevitably absorbed much of the strategic bandwidth of European leaders. This project aimed to offer a venue to connect short-term efforts and long-term consequences. In other words, it sought to accompany the frantic pace of crisis management with the in-depth assessment of the war's strategic repercussions. The purpose was to improve the capacity of the European Union to anticipate, and prepare for, possible developments down the line.

The project built on four foresight seminars, organised in cooperation with the partners that joined FEPS in supporting this important initiative – the Fondation Jean-Jaurés, the Olof Palme International Center and the Karl Renner Institute. These seminars engaged dozens of policymakers, experts and stakeholders from civil society and tackled the long-term implications of the war in Ukraine for key dimensions of international affairs. In particular, they addressed the geopolitics of energy and the green transition (September 2022), global governance and development (November 2022), trade and global supply chains (February 2023) and the future of armaments, disarmament and human security (April 2023).

The seminars applied a foresight methodology, structuring the debates around three basic clusters: identifying the main factors and actors shaping change in the long term; exploring the main uncertainties surrounding future developments, and the potential wild cards impacting them; and drawing implications for the EU. These thorough debates helped frame the project's research output, leading to an initial FEPS policy brief in February 2023: "*Terra incognita*: exploring the long-term implications of the war in Ukraine". This foresight report singled out three ways in which Russia's aggression affects long-term change, namely, as a big multiplier of earlier trends, a big disruption introducing major discontinuities and a big diversion that distracts from cooperation on shared global challenges. It concluded that "what lies ahead is *terra incognita* – a strategic landscape that eludes ready historical analogies".

The report set the stage for the final phase of the project, dedicated to mapping the uncharted strategic context that the war in Ukraine is moulding, as it intersects with structural trends and many other variables. Seven authoritative experts have been invited to share their assessment of the long-term impact of the war on topical issues on the European and global agendas. Each of them was asked to focus on aspects of continuity and discontinuity following the outbreak of the war, delineate potential developments and scenarios ahead in their respective fields, and outline policy implications for the EU. The resulting collection is a unique combination of knowledge, insight and policy-relevant conclusions concerning the reverberations of Russia's aggression over the next decade or so. As such, this is the first book reviewing the long-term implications of the war in Ukraine from a European perspective, and deriving priorities for EU action over the next 2024–2029 institutional cycle and beyond.

The chapters included in this book shed light on several dimensions of change and how they might impact Europe's security, prosperity, cohesion and integration. Andriy Korniychuk highlights the rise of the geopolitical paradigm, which is driving competition on the international stage, potentially leading to further instability, arms races and conflicts. As these risks are unlikely to dissipate soon, he notes the concurrent trend towards the "securitisation" of international affairs and domestic politics, and he argues that this trend needs careful this trend needs careful management to both cope with geopolitical turbulence and avoid marginalising other priorities. Korniychuk notes that the outcome of Russia's war in Ukraine will carry significant implications for the international order, including when it comes to preventing or deterring others from triggering military aggression. He calls on the EU to strengthen its role as a security provider by fostering the Common Security and Defence Policy and developing a "whole of society" approach to resilience. Domestic strength and cohesion will also help the EU to sustain multilateral dialogue and cooperation on common challenges, and to take a bold approach to the process of EU enlargement.

Thijs Van de Graaf and Thomas Pellerin-Carlin address one of the areas that have been more heavily impacted by Russia's aggression, namely, energy geopolitics and the future of the energy transition in Europe. In his chapter, Van de Graaf delineates the changing shape of the global energy map and how it might evolve in the future. He assesses the rerouting of energy flows and points to a mix of old and new vulnerabilities challenging energy security at the European and global levels. Van de Graaf concludes that, after the collapse of the EU–Russia energy partnership, the EU should beware of locking in dependence on other, more or less reliable, energy suppliers. The EU should instead punch its weight through joint energy purchases, double down on the energy transition and pursue a proactive energy diplomacy to ensure sustainable supply chains for the European Green Deal by partnering with other regions, such as Africa. Pellerin-Carlin argues that the great fossil fuel shock that hit Europe in 2021–2023 calls for a consequential response, on a scale adequate to the challenges ahead. He stresses various factors of European resilience in the face of crisis, such as the EU gas and electricity market, and various emerging challenges, including higher gas prices denting Europe's industrial competitiveness. In outlining scenarios ahead, Pellerin-Carlin notes that, despite some progress, there is a risk that the energy transition might fall prey to political polarisation and deadlock across Europe. He concludes that fostering the transition and sustaining Europe's green leadership requires crafting a massive, long-term climate investment plan and formulating a stronger, more inclusive narrative to back it up.

George Papaconstantinou, Elvrire Fabry and Annalisa Prizzon investigate the reverberations of the war in Ukraine across different dimensions of the international economic order, all of them stressing that the latter is at great risk of further weakening. Papaconstantinou finds evidence of many leaks in the plumbing of global economic interdependence and governance, and he focuses on the central issue of the long-term ramifications of the economic sanctions imposed by the West against Russia. While the emergence of viable alternatives to the current global financial infrastructure faces many obstacles, he argues that more countries will try to seek shelter from the weaponisation of finance by diversifying their networks. Papaconstantinou outlines a set of scenarios ranging from further fragmentation to the downright fracture of the global economic order. He argues that, in this context, the EU should further develop its "open strategic autonomy" and pursue a "derisking" approach. At the same time, Europeans should prevent geopolitical considerations from obliterating economic ones, they should better integrate their internal and external policies, and they should engage in reforming multilateralism.

Focusing on trade and investment, Fabry shares the analysis of an international system headed for different degrees of fragmentation and focuses on the systemic rivalry between the US and China as the principal factor leading in that direction. She reviews the main variables that will likely shape geoeconomic competition between the two superpowers, including the pace of China's rise and the risk of a clash around Taiwan. Fabry argues that Europeans are not in the driver's seat of the transformation of globalisation, but they are in the front line, facing related risks. They therefore need to devise an economic security strategy to defend their own interests, while taking into account Europe's stark reliance on external flows. Various strands of implementation of the EU's derisking agenda should be pursued alongside the strengthening of the single market, which remains Europe's main geoeconomic asset. Taking a global perspective, Prizzon argues that the combined impact of the Covid-19 pandemic and of Russia's aggression against Ukraine has severely strained the global development regime, setting back prospects for achieving the 2030 Sustainable Development Goals. She points to a growing gap in development finance and to the struggle for scarce resources amid competing spending priorities, from energy subsidies to defence. At the same time, development cooperation risks becoming another playground for strategic competition among great powers. Prizzon calls for addressing growing development challenges, and the related danger of debt distress in lower-income countries, before these crises deteriorate further. She finds that, among other measures, supporting the reform of multilateral development banks and providing them with adequate resources is a priority to deliver structural change through long-term investment.

The chapter by Daniela Schwarzer turns to the topical question of the implications of the war in Ukraine for the EU itself. Schwarzer stresses that Russia's aggression has redrawn the map of Europe, generating a new set of long-term challenges and opportunities for the EU. She outlines a range of risk factors potentially undermining economic growth and sociopolitical cohesion in Europe. These include the prospect of further economic divergence among member states polarising EU politics and making Europe more vulnerable to foreign interference. Schwarzer highlights two major questions that will define the future of Europe, namely, the prospects for EU enlargement and reform, and developments in the transatlantic partnership following the US presidential elections in 2024. On both issues, divisions among member states risk weakening the EU on the domestic and external fronts. Schwarzer concludes that designing a new European security order is a priority and that advancing the process of EU enlargement is a key part of that endeavour. At the same time, strengthening the democratic resilience of the EU and its member states will require enhancing their economic competitiveness and preserving social cohesion across the Union.

The final chapter of the book encapsulates some of the main findings of these contributions and of the wider FEPS project, looks into scenarios ahead, and offers additional guidelines for the EU's global agenda. In particular, it seeks to connect the impact of Russia's aggression of Ukraine to current trends, and to their potential evolution. This approach leads to sketching out three broad dimensions of change, and three pivotal "switch" factors that will affect the future of the international order. When surveying the emerging strategic landscape, which this project aimed to explore, the central finding is that the world faces a spiral of systemic regression. Backsliding entails the reversal of many of the political, security, economic and governance achievements of the last three decades, since the end of the Cold War. The relative rise or decline of individual powers is of course a critical metric of change in international affairs, but it is not the only one. This book stresses that the global stage on which all international actors, large and small, play is incrementally unravelling, whether in terms of geopolitical volatility, political polarisation, economic fragmentation, human insecurity or an ever-more-severe ecological crisis. In other words, there is a risk that Russia's war in Ukraine marks a tipping point, turning a world of relative progress, despite numerous setbacks and growing contestation, into one of lasting regression. That would be a paradigm change indeed.

This is not a prediction, but the assessment of a plausible, business-as-usual scenario – a scenario that appears worth stressing because the drivers that might bring it about are gaining in strength, number and speed. This book makes the case that being clear-eyed about the scenario of a regressive world is the first step to warding it off. Doing so requires deploying political leadership and strategic vision, grounded in the sobering analysis of the world as it is and of the trends shaping it, but aimed at revamping a global agenda of progress and cooperation. The central message of the book is that the EU should step up to the overarching strategic challenge of heading off a regressive world and trigger positive change, albeit under very difficult geopolitical conditions. Of course, the EU cannot succeed on its own, and frameworks of cooperation will vary, depending on the range of reliable partners on different agendas. However, few effective solutions to mitigate the challenges that are debasing the international order can be achieved without the strong commitment and co-leadership of the EU. Given the repercussions of the war in Ukraine for many aspects of international affairs, working with partners to repel Russia's aggression is not just a critical geopolitical requirement to protect Europe but also a central part of Europe's wider, global agenda.

The final chapter stresses that, to play a leading role in this global endeavour, the EU needs to strengthen its political fabric and power base at home. Over the next decade and beyond, the EU faces the twin challenges of deepening its integration while also striving to build a new European security architecture and pursue enlargement. The future of the transatlantic partnership with the US will be a key variable on both tracks. This book finds that, on a strategic level, different dimensions of EU power – geopolitical, normative and regulatory – are not alternative to each other but mutually reinforcing pillars of Europe as a viable power in a highly competitive and contested world. The question is whether these facets of EU power are properly integrated, and how they are mobilised. The book concludes that the EU needs to shift from firefighting (crisis management) to forest management, which requires devising comprehensive, long-term approaches to confront systemic challenges and, when needed, challengers. This applies across the board, from economic governance to defence policies, various aspects of EU resilience and the stabilisation of wider Europe. The EU needs to shape up as a stronger global power to be a stronger advocate of a progressive agenda, and to avert a regressive world.

Andriy Korniychuk

1 | Geopolitical crossroads: the strategic landscape after Russia's invasion of Ukraine

The global strategic and security landscape is undergoing a structural revision to adapt to the challenges that have emerged since the start of Russia's full-scale invasion of Ukraine. A war of this magnitude magnifies and exacerbates existing challenges while also generating new ones. The number of conflicts was rising, and their drivers spreading, prior to the outbreak of all-out war in Ukraine in 2022. In its latest 2023 yearbook report the Stockholm International Peace Research Institute (SIPRI) mentions the staggering number of 56 armed conflicts around the world.[1] It is no surprise that, in such a security environment, global military expenditure grew for the eighth consecutive year (for example, in Europe, expenditure grew by 13% from 2021 to 2022, while, on average, governments worldwide spent 6.2% of their budgets on the military).[2] In Europe itself, a "ring of fire" superseded the aspiration to establish a "ring of friends" around the European Union. Russia's renewed, full-scale aggression towards Ukraine exacerbated this trend and dismantled the European security order.

Should James Carville, political adviser to Bill Clinton in the 1992 presidential election, be asked to reflect on the key issue driving the strategic agenda in 2023 and for the foreseeable future, he might proclaim: "It's geopolitics, stupid!"[3] Russia's aggression against Ukraine underscored the importance of geopolitics as a key dimension shaping international

---

1   SIPRI (2023) *SIPRI Yearbook 2023: Armaments, Disarmament and International Security* (Oxford University Press) (https://www.sipri.org/yearbook/2023).
2   Ibid.
3   In the 1992 US presidential campaign, James Carville famously coined the popular slogan "It's the economy, stupid" to underline the importance of the economy for American voters.

relations and as a framework for analysing the behaviour of political actors and their strategic choices. The following sections provide an analysis of this broader shift through an assessment of the emerging (dis)continuities and trends and an overview of the actors and factors shaping change, followed by an outline of potential bifurcations and developments ahead and recommendations for the EU to prepare for the (un)certain future.

Europe in a changing security paradigm

Experts have accurately pointed out that, after Russia's renewed aggression, the definition of Ukraine as a "buffer state" between the West and Russia started losing its relevance.[4] Even if there is by now a consensus that Ukraine's place is with NATO and the EU, de jure membership of NATO might not be a near-term prospect for Ukraine, as the final statement of NATO's Vilnius Summit indicated.[5] In a similar vein, accession to the EU is a very demanding and resource-intensive process. Yet, de facto, with every month of resistance against Russia, every new batch of military assistance, and every reform on the paths to EU and NATO accession, Ukraine is advancing its integration into the Western political and security architecture. Ukraine can be considered pivotal to an effective and sustainable model for the European postwar security order. The reconfiguration of the latter has started quickly in response to Russia's aggression. Finland has joined NATO and Sweden is in the process of doing so, while Denmark has opted for joining the EU's Common Security and Defence Policy. Room for neutrality or strategic ambiguity is rapidly closing.

With the Western camp consolidating in the face of Russia's threat, the prospect of a new Iron Curtain in Europe is looming. It remains uncertain whether the same process will unfold elsewhere in the world. The debate surrounding the war in Ukraine has demonstrated that an increasing number of countries, from Africa and Latin America to the Middle East and Asia, entertain growing ambitions of foreign policy autonomy

---

4   Biscop, S. (2023) "War for Ukraine and the rediscovery of geopolitics: must the EU draw new battlelines or keep an open door?" Egmont Paper 123, June (https://www.egmontinstitute.be/war-for-ukraine-and-the-rediscovery-of-geopolitics/).

5   NATO (2023) "Vilnius Summit communiqué". Press release, 11 July (https://www.nato.int/cps/en/natohq/official_texts_217320.htm).

and do not wish to align with the front of countries countering Russia. The outcome of the war in Ukraine and its aftermath will determine if the curtain falls on Europe. It will also be a critical variable defining whether the geopolitical fracture determined by the war in Europe will be mainly confined to the continent or drive rivalry on a global scale.

The US-led North Atlantic Alliance has been a defining feature of the security and defence architecture of the collective West since the end of World War II. Russia's unprovoked attack on Ukraine confirmed Washington's foundational role as a security provider for its allies and partners in Europe. Cooperation between the US and its allies has been remarkable in response to the full-scale war in Ukraine. However, Washington's renewed commitment under the Biden administration to Europe's security in the face of war raised other questions, such as the political sustainability of Europe's (over)reliance on the US as a security guarantor. In a confrontational strategic landscape, such a situation could become very challenging for Washington's partners should armed conflicts requiring US engagement simultaneously erupt in different regions of the world. Moreover, the Trump administration has already demonstrated that Europe's place on Washington's priority list can drastically change – a daunting prospect that cannot be ruled out following the 2024 presidential elections in the US. What is clear is that, in the short to medium term, Washington's role as the centrepiece of any emerging peace and security architecture in Europe is more likely to be challenged by the political processes inside the country or by developments in other regions, notably the Indo-Pacific, than by its European partners and allies.

On Europe's side, the brutality of Russia's onslaught on Ukraine has triggered a revision of threat perceptions and of plans to boost military capabilities. This process has prompted a reflection on core principles and ideas behind security and defence strategies on the national and multilateral levels (notably NATO and the EU). As a result, renewed focus has been placed on military deterrence as an essential component of strategic stability. In a reset of its long-term deterrence and defence policies (at the 2022 Madrid and 2023 Vilnius summits), NATO has recognised Russia as the most significant direct threat to its security. The Alliance has already responded to the threat with more forward-deployed troops and prepositioned equipment on its eastern flank. In case of attack, it has put larger contingents at a high-readiness level for quick response. Further ramping-up of investments in defence capabilities is increasingly presented as a sine qua non condition for rendering the cost of confrontation unacceptable for a potential aggressor. In other words, the stage is set for what could become a new arms race.

The EU, a peacebuilding project at its core, has been facing a momentous geostrategic paradigm shift and has responded by upgrading its threat assessment, its narrative and, to some extent, its geopolitical posture. It remains unclear how this evolution fits with the long-overriding priority of the EU and its member states to build a multilateral order and manage global interdependence by creating mutually beneficial long-term partnerships. A decade ago, in 2012, the Union received the Nobel Prize "for over six decades of contribution to the advancement of peace and reconciliation, democracy and human rights in Europe".[6] At that time, the feeling prevailed that military aggression in Europe as an instrument for dealing with disputes and disagreements had come close to being, to quote the Schuman Declaration, "not merely unthinkable, but materially impossible".[7]

The shift of the EU's posture towards that of a soft power with hard edges[8] started well before the outbreak of full-scale war in Ukraine in 2022. Russia's aggression of Ukraine in 2014, growing global strategic competition driven by China's rise, and ongoing political-military turbulence across Europe's neighbourhood and Africa were among the factors significantly contributing to such a shift in perceptions and, incrementally, policies. However, the EU continued to tread water lightly, with modest increases in defence budgets across the member states and limited foreign deployments, consisting predominantly of civilian crisis-management and military training missions (for example, to the Sahel).[9]

Russia's all-out aggression against Ukraine has decisively prompted Brussels to sharpen its hard edges. This process is likely to progress incrementally, yet with tangible results. On a strategic level, the adoption

---

6 See https://www.nobelprize.org/prizes/peace/2012/summary/.

7 See https://european-union.europa.eu/principles-countries-history/history-eu/1945-59/schuman-declaration-may-1950_en.

8 Goldthau, A., and Sitter, N. (2015) "Soft power with a hard edge: EU policy tools and energy security". *Review of International Political Economy*, 22(5): 941–965. Moreover, Joseph S. Nye, one of the most renowned theorists of (soft) power, has argued in his works for the importance of combining hard and soft power (the so-called smart-power approach) to be truly effective and influential in contemporary world affairs. This is why it is so crucial for the EU to develop hard edges around its soft-power core.

9 Fiot, D. (2022) "A path to 2030: how can the 'Strategic Compass' help protect Europe?" *Progressive Post* 18, FEPS (https://progressivepost.eu/wp-content/uploads/PP18.pdf).

of the EU's Strategic Compass[10] or the latest iteration of the Strategic Foresight Reports by the European Commission[11] are reflective of the ongoing paradigm shift. While covering different policy ground, both reflect a clear sense of urgency to respond to renewed large-scale war in Europe and its far-reaching transnational consequences. In terms of concrete measures, the adoption of the Act in Support of Ammunition Production (ASAP) and the mobilisation of the European Peace Facility to provide lethal equipment (as well as nonlethal support) for Ukraine are among the visible indicators of the winds of change.

Most EU member states have announced major increases in defence expenditure, which are expected to amount to €70 billion in additional spending across the EU over the next three years.[12] At the same time, European policymakers will have to invest additional resources to ensure the competitiveness of the European defence industry. It remains to be seen whether national defence planning processes can be better coordinated to strengthen Europe's defence industrial base, as opposed to largely buying off-the-shelf weapon systems from abroad.[13] Contracts in the Netherlands, Denmark, Romania and Poland have already gone to Israeli, Turkish and South Korean companies. Poland, to take only one example, is expected to buy Abrams tanks, F-35 fighters, and advanced rockets and rocket launchers worth $10 billion from the US.[14] These recent developments are reflective of the fact that military industries in member states are ill-prepared to meet the demands of wartime. In addition, considering the impeding feeling of insecurity, for many EU member states the top priority remains to enhance the American security engagement in Europe.

---

10   Council of the European Union (2022) "A Strategic Compass for a stronger EU security and defence in the next decade". Press release, 21 March (https://www.consilium.europa.eu/en/press/press-releases/2022/03/21/a-strategic-compass-for-a-stronger-eu-security-and-defence-in-the-next-decade/).

11   European Commission (2023) "2023 Strategic Foresight Report: sustainability and people's wellbeing at the heart of Europe's Open Strategic Autonomy". COM(2023) 376, July (https://commission.europa.eu/document/download/f8f67d33-194c-4c89-a4a6-795980a1dabd_en?filename=SFR-23_en.pdf).

12   Boswinkel, L. (2023) "Taking stock: Europe's rearmament, one year on". CSDS Policy Brief 08/2023, Brussels School of Governance, 15 March (https://prod-b4156475194d8706-vub.paddlecms.net/sites/default/files/2023-03/CSDS%20Policy%20brief_2308.pdf).

13   Biscop, S. (2023) "War for Ukraine and the rediscovery of geopolitics".

14   Martin, P., and McBride, C. (2023) "US plans to sell Poland $10 billion in Himars rocket launchers and ammunition". *Bloomberg*, 7 February (https://www.bloomberg.com/news/articles/2023-02-07/us-to-sell-poland-10-billion-in-himars-ammunition).

Beyond the broadly defined Western coalition, the response to Russia's blatant violation of international norms has been quite restrained. In a war with a clear aggressor, some countries around the globe proposed solutions that sought to appease the perpetrator. From a Western perspective, such a situation represents a continuation of some historical patterns. Since the times of the Soviet Union, Moscow's propaganda machine has used anticolonial and anti-imperialist rhetoric in the Global South to build up the image of Russia as a champion of those who suffer from Western (neo)colonialism. This ideological underpinning has been further strengthened in more recent years through economic, cultural, educational and military diplomacy. As a result, criticism of Moscow's invasion, framed as a preventive strike against Western (military) expansionism, has been somewhat muted.

At the same time, Russia has tightened its relations with those who strive to gain more influence in the alleged Western-dominated international system. After the 2022 invasion, formats such as the BRICS (Brazil, Russia, India, China and South Africa) are increasingly used to elaborate and propel an alternative proposition to alleged Western dominance in international affairs. China's Xi Jinping, during his 2023 visit to Moscow, hailed the current state of international affairs as entailing "changes the likes of which we haven't seen for 100 years". Yet the fact that external military support for Russia's invasion has been relatively modest (except in the case of Iran) confirms that the rhetorical anti-Western camp is mainly driven by opportunistic motives. Russia's partnerships are marriages of convenience, which will persist as long as their costs and risks do not outweigh the benefits for Moscow's partners.

One notable discontinuity marked by the war is the fact that Russia has been exhausting its military resources due to Ukraine's effective resistance. Such a situation may soon lead to a geopolitical vacuum in its traditional regions of influence (Central Asia and Caucasia) and impact the ongoing multipolar competition in the Middle East, the Sahel, and sub-Saharan Africa. China and Turkey have already started exploring this geostrategic opening. Notably, Turkey has used Russia's invasion of Ukraine to overtly pursue a posture of strategic autonomy in multiple theatres. From the beginning of the full-scale war, Ankara has striven to become the main mediator between the West and Russia, using its geographical location and its status as a NATO member to help broker solutions between conflicting sides (for example, the Black Sea grain deal).

In sum, Russia's war of aggression has had a broad and diverse impact on the geostrategic landscape – accelerating and magnifying, while simultaneously changing and disrupting, many existing trends. On a more conceptual level, it (re)opened the discussions around the very definition of security and the conditions that are necessary to uphold it. While marking the return of a large-scale conventional military conflict in Europe, the war has also underscored the centrality of nontraditional and nonmilitary threats to the current and future security agenda. The conduct of the war has exposed the variety of battlefields where contemporary warfare takes place: information and the digital domain, critical infrastructures, supply chains, energy, and the sociodemographic dimension do not exhaust the list.[15]

In particular, the successful resistance of Ukraine has underscored the importance of cross-societal resistance.[16] In addition to the military component of defence and deterrence, a "whole of society approach"[17] to security is very likely to garner further interest around the globe. Lessons learned from the ongoing war in Ukraine can be expected to find their way into revised security doctrines. Since 2022, many governments have shown a heightened interest in certain types of military equipment, such as unmanned aerial vehicles (UAV), loitering munitions (kamikaze drones) or air defence systems.[18] On top of that, more investment can be expected in volunteer defence structures (patterned after Ukrainian volunteer battalions or formations such as the Lithuanian National

---

15 This is why the German government (among others), in its first ever published security strategy, released in June 2023, refers to the integrated approach to security, drawing attention to the availability of resources, energy security, climate change, health and disinformation. See "The National Security Strategy: providing guidance in the face of current and foreseeable security challenges", Federal Ministry of Defence website (https://www.bmvg.de/en/national-security-policy).

16 Hanna Shelest, renowned Ukrainian security expert, notes that cross-society resilience in Ukraine entailed bringing all military and security agencies under a single command, assisted by support from the civilian population. She sees the transformation of the Ukrainian army as rooted in upgrading logistics and communications and empowering mid-level officers. Furthermore, the authorities have put in place a network of reservists and taken measures to ensure Ukrainian society's broader resilience to crises. See Shelest, H. (2022) "Defend. Resist. Repeat: Ukraine's lessons for European defence". Policy brief, European Council on Foreign Relations, November; https://ecfr.eu/publication/defend-resist-repeat-ukraines-lessons-for-european-defence/.

17 Such an approach is partially represented in the total-defence doctrines of Nordic and Baltic counties, Switzerland, and Singapore.

18 For example, the establishment of the European Sky Shield Initiative, which entails multinational acquisition and integration of a broad range of air defence capabilities, currently by a group of 17 European countries.

Defence Volunteer Forces), cyber-brigades (and cyber-defence in general) and plans to modernise state border-guard services (for example, with advanced technological surveillance systems and stronger physical protection). The explosions on the Nord Stream II pipeline and the constant, purposeful Russian attacks on Ukraine's critical infrastructure further illustrated the importance of effective protection of such infrastructure. In response, NATO has already launched a centre for protecting undersea pipelines and cables.[19]

Shapers and drivers of competition

From Moscow's failed blitzkrieg, to its war of attrition in Ukraine and mutiny in the ranks of the Wagner group, there is high uncertainty around the future course of the war and its outcome. The latter is among the most important factors shaping developments in the strategic and security domains down the line. The terms under which Ukraine and Russia will cease hostilities will impact the moves of other actors on the "grand chessboard", with consequences spanning well beyond Europe. The question of Russia's future is one of the most perplexing. Whether Russia should and ultimately can be incorporated into the future European security order will have a decisive impact on that order's shape and further development. The current prospects for this outcome are bleak, since it would require a radical change in Russia's current geopolitical agenda and much successive confidence-building, which appears impossible under the current leadership. Furthermore, a strategic consensus must be reached regarding the understanding of what sustainable peace in Ukraine (and in Europe) entails. A ceasefire followed by negotiations for a peace deal may offer a much-needed (re)solution to high-intensity war, yet only the end of Russia's current neoimperialistic designs would offer a permanent exit from the spiral of insecurity and instability in Europe.

The response to Russia's invasion of Ukraine has amplified the US–China rivalry, making the prospect of a revival of Cold War-like dynamics more tangible. The possibility of increasingly hostile relations spilling over from the economic to the military domain (for example, over Taiwan) could be a turning point in international relations, with massive consequences. Given

---

19   Cook, L. (2023) "NATO moves to protect undersea pipelines, cables as concern mounts over Russian sabotage threat". *PBS News Hour*, 16 June (https://www.pbs.org/newshour/world/nato-moves-to-protect-undersea-pipelines-cables-as-concern-mounts-over-russian-sabotage-threat).

the consequences witnessed in the wake of Russia's full-scale invasion of Ukraine, a US–China military confrontation would surely disrupt global supply chains, hinder international trade and destabilise financial markets on an unprecedented scale. It would trigger a global economic crisis and a serious recession, and produce a devastating shock to the multilateral order. The grim prospect of confrontational power politics leading to bloc formation has already motivated an increasing number of countries, from Asia to Africa and Latin America, to pursue an autonomous foreign policy and escape full alignment with either camp. Turkey's energetic pursuit of strategic autonomy in foreign policy has already affected the reconfiguration of the geopolitical space in Europe and neighbouring regions, with Ankara seeking to establish itself as an indispensable actor on many dossiers.[20] Whether middle powers will choose (or be compelled) to align their foreign policies to those of the great powers, or will walk a "third way", will have a considerable impact on the trajectory of the international order (bipolarity v. multipolarity).

The trends shaping regional and global geopolitics cannot be delinked from domestic political developments, which in turn affect the priorities of powers large and small on the international stage. Already before the Covid-19 pandemic, the political resilience of long-standing democracies had been put under unprecedented pressure. An increasingly confrontational and insecure international environment serves the narratives of nationalist political forces on the ideological spectrum's far right and heightens the dangers of interference by malicious foreign actors. Resilience against democratic backsliding will be a critical factor in shaping future developments in the security and strategic domains. In this context, one should not neglect the durability of populist and illiberal movements,[21] the general trend towards the mainstreaming of the far right, and the pull that the latter increasingly exercises on traditional conservative political forces, which are compelled (or persuaded) to take over some of their slogans. An upcoming major test of resilience is expected to take place during the 2024 presidential elections in the United States. A potential return of Donald Trump to the White House could have a seismic effect

---

20   For example, Ankara's imposing additional conditions on Finland and Sweden to join NATO, its reluctance to side with the EU on sanctions against Russia, and its role in the Black Sea grain deal and in the resolution of the war over Nagorno-Karabakh.

21   For example, the popularity of Trumpism, the reelection of Erdoğan in Turkey, the riots caused by Bolsonaro's supporters in Brazil, the prosecution of Raul Gandhi in India, Orbán's victory in elections against democratic opposition in Hungary, and civil unrest in Georgia.

on the domestic front, with major repercussions for the shape of the strategic and security landscape far beyond Washington.

Technology is likely to be a game-changer at all levels of politics, governance, security and strategic competition at large. A race to develop next-generation capabilities in the land, naval, air, cyber and space domains was already underway prior to 2022. In its war against Ukraine, Russia conducts military operations using both outdated equipment and cutting-edge weapons. While Moscow possesses considerable technological capabilities (particularly in the military sector), widespread corruption, brain drain and unprecedented Western sanctions seriously undermine its contention for technological primacy. The latter is quickly becoming the principal domain where the US–China rivalry plays out. The rapid evolution of artificial intelligence (AI) in particular promises to open several Pandora's boxes. On a strategic level, due to unprecedented capacity for data aggregation and analysis, AI drastically changes the way security-related decisions will be made. It significantly improves the capabilities to predict and anticipate, while at the same time raising questions about the legitimacy and legality of preemptive lethal action. On a (hard) security level, technological evolution will impact the speed and freedom of action on the battlefield. Yet from a values-based and human-centred perspective, it raises controversial questions about the legitimate, lawful usage of autonomous systems in military operations.[22]

Not only the military balance but the balance of global power will critically depend on who will be able to harness the new technology and exercise control over specialised, advanced hardware used for training AI.[23] The latter will depend on the possession of vast technical and financial resources, as well as data. At the moment, containing the private-sector-driven development of ever-more-advanced forms of AI appears to be an uphill battle. If so, however, then innovative and inclusive forms of governance of the new technology will be essential to steering an ordered transition into a new technological age. Equally important is whether societies will be able to maximise the advantages of the AI while minimising the risks of its usage.

---

22 McChrystal, S., and Roy, A. (2023) "AI has entered the situation room". *Foreign Policy*, 19 June (https://foreignpolicy.com/2023/06/19/ai-artificial-intelligence-national-security-foreign-policy-threats-prediction/).

23 Scharre, P. (2023) "AI's gatekeepers aren't prepared for what's coming". *Foreign Policy*, 19 June (https://foreignpolicy.com/2023/06/19/ai-regulation-development-us-china-competition-technology/).

Geopolitical turbulence: bracing for uncertainty

The analysis in this chapter points to an existential question, which will frame the future of the strategic and security landscape: are actors on the "grand chessboard" already preparing for an inevitable (military) confrontation? Is Thucydides's trap unavoidable?[24] Will there be space to address unfolding issues such as climate crises through international cooperation? Will multilateral institutions have the clout to foster international cooperation in the absence of leadership and direction from the great powers? The outcome of Russia's war against Ukraine will certainly shed more light on the way forward. Moscow's ultimate and definitive defeat, accompanied by the collapse of the current regime, commitment to arms control, and democratic reforms, would send a powerful message about the resolute unity and resilience of the democratic world against an attack on international law and institutions. It would show that modern-day democracies have teeth and can bite back in their defence. As a ripple effect, it could discourage others from embarking on a revisionist and aggressive path in foreign policy for the foreseeable future.

Conversely, protracted confrontation between the West and Russia, during and after the war in Ukraine, would likely compound the prospect of systemic competition and rising tensions among great powers. This may or may not entail more military conflicts. As argued above, the very understanding of security and deterrence is undergoing comprehensive revision. As a result, even a scenario in which conflicts are fewer and less intensive than the current war in Ukraine does not rule out the possibility of permanent confrontation on other levels, through geoeconomic means and cyber-hybrid warfare.

Most of the alternative scenarios to Russia's defeat are likely to include concessions on the part of Ukraine, which would represent the West's failure to uphold international law and stand its ground against aggression. This setback would come on top of an already sobering track record of unsuccessful interventions in the Middle East, Afghanistan and Africa. Certainly, after two years of largely unsuccessful military campaigns, in any scenario the Kremlin is almost sure to exit the battlefield militarily wounded, economically crippled and internationally discredited. Yet Moscow could still declare victory should Ukraine's path

---

24 The term, popularised by American political scientist Graham T. Allison, sees war as the most likely outcome when an emerging power threatens to displace an existing one. Most recently, it has been widely used in reference to a potential confrontation between the US (the old power) and China (the emerging power).

to NATO membership, which entails for Kyiv the most comprehensive set of security guarantees, be indefinitely postponed. And, with a nuclear arsenal ready to launch at the push of a button, and its vast natural and human resources, a resentful and wounded Russia would remain a major security threat.

Hence, the more Moscow gains from the war, despite unprecedented sanctions, overwhelming losses, and the proven incompetence of its military-political elites, the more its example might embolden other like-minded countries to resort to similar measures, or at least to distance themselves from the West. In that case, there would be a significant chance of the emergence of a multipolar global order characterised by bloc formation and consolidation around geographical borders and geo-political concerns, with power politics prevailing over efforts to pursue multilateral cooperation. As a result, economic deterrence measures (such as forging and manipulating interdependence) would be increasingly complemented by military ones (a strong military posture, accompanied by the capability to inflict major damage across all domains, such as cyber and space).

The multilateral order is unlikely to persist in its current form in most scenarios.[25] The cracks are apparent. Since Russia's renewed aggression in 2022, the Organization for Security and Co-operation in Europe has barely had a role in bringing about a peaceful resolution to the unfathomable tragedy in Ukraine. The African Union, the G5 Sahel and the Economic Community of West African States do not have an effective answer to the rise of jihadism, pervasive coups d'état and the infiltration of Russian mercenaries on the continent. The diplomatic measures from the Association of Southeast Asian Nations have brought no resolution to the dire situation in Myanmar. Finally, the war underscored the importance of the UN in humanitarian diplomacy and its key role for the provision and coordination of development aid. At the same time, the fact of Russia's assuming the presidency of the UN Security Council while intent on invading a sovereign country marks a setback for the credibility of that body and speaks of the inescapable difficulty of the UN to adapt to the changing strategic and security landscape.

That said, the complete unravelling of multilateralism does not seem the most plausible scenario, because such an outcome would send

---

25   Puglierin, J. (2023) "Multilateral changes: turn and face the strange". Commentary, European Council on Foreign Relations, 12 July (https://ecfr.eu/article/multilateral-chapeau/).

destructive shockwaves through advanced and developing countries alike, as well as all the major powers. The controversy about the response to the Covid-19 pandemic and the global vaccination campaign, the global food crisis triggered by Russia's invasion of Ukraine and the ongoing impact of climate change underscore the fragility of the multilateral order. This is well understood not only in Brussels, Berlin, Paris, London and Washington but also in Ankara, Abu Dhabi, Beijing, Brasilia and New Delhi. This is why there is a long-running debate about the reform, not the dismantling, of the multilateral order, despite its deficits. Ultimately, progress may be achievable in some areas more than others, leading to a patchwork of deeper and looser regimes in different domains.

Another development cutting across different scenarios is the impact of the ongoing polycrisis on the process of securitisation of international affairs and domestic politics. This consists of the extension of the number of policy areas being framed through security categories and narratives that call for, and legitimise, extraordinary measures to protect against threats and challenges. The current debate on "economic security" is an instance of this larger trend. However, securitisation is a double-edged sword – the way in which it will be managed will determine its impact.

A transparent and accountable system of checks and balances is key to ensuring that security-driven measures improve the resilience of (supra)national democratic systems against malign foreign actors without affecting their foundations. The resilience of society to withstand hybrid threats and the preservation of critical infrastructure against attacks or sabotage are indispensable elements for effectively upholding security and political stability. The "whole of society" and total-defence approaches to security have already proved their value as an integral feature of future defence doctrines. Yet, in a post-truth era filled with hybrid warfare, securitisation can also be instrumentalised to promote narratives and justify policies and decisions that lead to the concentration of power, democratic backsliding and breaches of citizen's rights. In the coming years, it will be crucial to strike the right balance between, on the one hand, the necessary measures to enhance defence and broader resilience and, on the other, the preservation of an open society and of all categories of individual rights from the risk of encroachment by state authorities on security grounds. Whether democratic oversight and a sound, inclusive public debate shape this trend or the latter spins out of control and takes the form of hypersecuritisation will make a big difference to the quality of politics and democracy.

This dimension of change is accompanied by the militarisation of international affairs – a trend that is not expected to subside soon. The heightened state of military preparedness is intended to serve as the ultimate deterrence factor, making aggression too costly for the perpetrator. Yet one must wonder whether the metaphor of Chekhov's gun might not at some point be applied to the strategic and security landscape.[26] A growing arsenal of increasingly sophisticated arms, predestined to fire, either purposefully or by mistake, risks making military confrontation in one region of the world or another a matter of time. The last section of this chapter outlines some of the measures that the EU can take to cope with risks and threats while seeking to promote a less confrontational international environment. These recommendations are grouped according to three dimensions – global, regional and internal.

A comprehensive EU response to geopolitical challenges

The global dimension

A more hostile geostrategic reality requires a more pragmatic, sober, but nevertheless determined approach to sustain multilateralism. Brussels must refrain from replicating unilateral and protectionist measures, except where essential to protect the EU's core interests. The EU should not follow other powers in a sheer competition for seizing markets and resources but strive to shape more appealing offers that bridge the short-term needs and long-term priorities of partners. Otherwise, a tug-of-war over exclusive spheres of influence will intensify. Furthermore, the EU should continue to leverage the fact that China and various other rising powers are embedded in the (weakening) global economic order to keep them part of the system. The EU is not in control of their ascendancy to power, but it can seek to shape the conditions under which it unfolds and help set the scene for (de)escalation. This is an increasingly demanding and contested approach, given the underlying tensions straining relations between China, the US and Europe, and global geopolitics at large, but the costs of failure suggest that it is worth pursuing.

Multilateral engagement should not be abandoned even in highly contested areas. Moscow's resorting to nuclear blackmail to advance

---

26 Chekhov's gun is a literary technique, a narrative device. It presupposes that any object that appears in the story should have a certain significance. Hence, if a gun is described hanging on the wall, the expectation is that it is going to be used at some point.

its political agenda and military goals has once again underscored the topicality of pursuing arms control, disarmament and nonproliferation efforts. The consequence of a global (nuclear) arms race could be catastrophic. The geopolitical and security conditions described in this chapter compound proliferation risks. While preparing to respond to geopolitical threats, the EU should also work to preserve the fabric of dialogue in this domain with all those not engaging in aggression. By keeping channels open and exploring confidence-building measures, the EU would pave the way for deescalation when the right conditions arise. In the meantime, efforts must continue to strengthen international law and norms in order to address the impact and risks associated with the use of nuclear weapons, not least from a humanitarian perspective. Moreover, as for the pressing need to set legal, ethical and moral boundaries on the use of autonomous weapon systems, the EU should actively participate in this process. This is part of a wider effort to be at the forefront of human-centric and ethical development of AI in Europe and on the global stage (through, for example, the European AI Act). In a race against time, the EU should press fast-forward to incorporate AI into its strategic and security thinking. International cooperation and cybersecurity measures will be crucial to tame the exponential pace of this technology and prevent or contain its weaponisation.

The regional dimension

In the new geopolitical reality, the EU's enlargement process must be viewed as an integral element of Europe's peace and security architecture. The current modalities of the accession process are no longer adequate to the geopolitical challenges the EU faces in its east. On a conceptual level, the EU needs a more progressive philosophy – a political, empathic approach that focuses on strategic engagement and partnership (not strategic ambiguity), guided by a long-term calculus of the strategic benefits of enlargement (not short-term political objections). On a practical level, it requires credible incentives with sufficient financial backing, allowing for sustained policy convergence and leading to a merit-based, staged integration into the EU.[27]

---

27   Korniychuk, A. (2023) "The case of Ukraine's candidacy to the EU: progressive policy towards the eastern neighbourhood as a cornerstone of the EU's stability and security". FEPS Policy Study, March (https://feps-europe.eu/publication/the-case-of-ukraines-can didacy-to-the-eu/).

To boost its geopolitical prowess and to improve the stability and security of the wider European neighbourhood, the EU must prioritise enlargement over looser forms of cooperation with its partners, and reevaluate or dismiss the formats that are no longer fit for purpose (such as the Eastern Partnership). The European Political Community can remain part of the EU's foreign policy toolkit, yet its goal should be to offer a platform for its members to improve cooperation and exchange of good practices, while tackling geopolitical tensions in the EU's neighbourhood. Importantly, such formats should not be used as a substitute for actual EU membership, trapping countries in a geopolitical and legal-institutional limbo, even if they can help support candidate countries on their path towards EU accession.

The internal dimension

The EU must strive to elevate its role as a security provider. The EU should develop further incentives for the development of the European defence technology and industrial base and boost the intra-EU coordination of national defence planning. It should also strengthen the resilience of relevant supply chains (infrastructure, raw materials) and attract a skilled workforce to deal effectively with potential bottlenecks. In line with the above, Brussels should look into expanding the resources available for the European Defence Fund. Over time, and in parallel with advancing towards a shared approach to armament exports, the EU should consider developing a similar instrument to the US government's Foreign Military Sales programme,[28] thus pursuing more effective defence diplomacy, improving the defence capabilities of partners, and allowing the domestic defence industry to benefit from comprehensive, long-term partnerships. The Strategic Compass must receive sufficient financial and political backing during the implementation phase of its ambitious agenda. Finally, the growing application of the European Peace Facility in the EU's external action must be accompanied by an increase in the transparency, oversight and accountability pertaining to the EU's off-budget instruments.

European security will depend on a comprehensive approach to resilience. To succeed, the EU must internalise a "whole of society",

---

28 The programme represents a comprehensive approach to security partnerships by the US government. It allows approved foreign governments to purchase a wide range of defence items, including military equipment, weapons, ammunition, spare parts and related services from the US. Such an approach boosts the capabilities of partners while supporting the development of military industry in the US.

human-centred approach. Sophisticated military tech is no substitute for societal resilience against hybrid warfare and malign foreign influence. Activities to be expanded on a wider European scale (with tailoring to specific individual, regional or national circumstances) may include developing tools for digital resilience; promotion of systematic, cross-institutional response to hybrid threats; adapting civic and media education to emerging trends; support for independent, quality media and further investment in improving capacities for strategic and crisis communications; and training on cognitive security and disinformation psychology targeted at media professionals, civil society and opinion leaders, politicians, policymakers, and government officials.[29]

The EU and its member states should not abandon the pursuit of European strategic autonomy – their ability to define and achieve EU priorities while decreasing their dependence on others. At the same time, they should take a pragmatic approach. On defence, Europeans should take more responsibility for their security and that of neighbouring regions, in ways that complement the role of NATO. The Alliance will provide the foundation of collective defence for the foreseeable future, short of major twists in US politics and strategic posture, but, under NATO's New Force Model, Europeans will have a much larger role to play in upgrading the defence of Europe.[30] At the same time, the EU should build on those areas of the security agenda where it has distinct experience and resources, such as conflict prevention, mediation, postconflict peacebuilding, and resilience-building cybersecurity and energy security.[31] A comprehensive peace and security agenda plays to Europe's strengths and is critical to both Europe's security and that of its partners.

With Russia's war against Ukraine, the European security order in tatters and power politics on the rise on the global stage, Europe's strategic context is such that security and defence issues are going to remain high on the agenda for the foreseeable future. This is why the EU needs a socially responsible, progressive approach to manage the security and

---

29 Teperik, D. (2022) "Resilience against disinformation: a new Baltic way to follow?" Report, International Centre for Defence and Security, October (https://icds.ee/en//download/47066871/).

30 Biscop, S. (2022) "The New Force Model: NATO's European army?" Egmont Policy Brief 285, September (https://www.egmontinstitute.be/the-new-force-model-natos-european-army/).

31 Juncos, A. E. (2023) "Elevating the EU's added value as a security provider". FEPS Policy Brief, European Strategic Autonomy series – Security and Defence (https://feps-europe.eu/publication/848-elevating-the-eus-added-value-as-a-security-provider/).

defence agenda, in a way that connects with, and does not displace, other goals central to Europe's future (such as the green transition, the reform of the EU's economic governance, technological innovation and adequate investment in public services). That requires an open, inclusive debate, as well as action to mutually reinforce defence, economic, social, technological and ecological objectives. In particular, emerging challenges have underscored the importance of cohesion policies as key elements of social resilience in Europe. Therefore, the EU should become a more geopolitical actor not at the cost of other priorities but by advancing them under a larger strategic approach.

Thijs Van de Graaf

2 | The geopolitics of energy after Russia's war in Ukraine

Russia's brutal invasion of Ukraine has shaken the foundations of the global energy system, triggering the "first truly global energy crisis"[1] and reshaping the geopolitical landscape. As the world grapples with the fallout from this crisis, it is becoming increasingly clear that the energy sector will be one of the sectors most heavily impacted by the conflict. The ongoing reconfiguration of the energy map could well surpass the reshuffling of energy markets that occurred in the aftermath of the 1970s oil crises.[2]

This chapter provides an in-depth assessment of how Russia's war in Ukraine will impact the global energy agenda in the long term. It examines how the conflict has reshaped the energy landscape and explores the emerging trends in energy geopolitics. Furthermore, it investigates the potential scenarios for the future of global energy politics, identifying the opportunities and challenges on the path to a sustainable and secure energy future.

A new energy map

Russia and Europe's energy divorce

The war in Ukraine has brought about a seismic shift in global energy politics. The most significant outcome of the war has been the disruption of the long-standing energy "marriage" between Europe and Russia. For years, Russia had been Europe's dominant supplier of fossil fuels, and even the annexation of Crimea in 2014 did not alter this dynamic. Yet

---
1   IEA (2022) "World energy outlook 2022". Report, Paris, OECD/IEA, October, p. 3.
2   Marques, C. F., and Fickling, D. (2023) "The year that redrew the energy map". *Bloomberg*, 26 February.

the 2022 full-scale invasion proved a breaking point. The EU, alongside other Western countries, has implemented sweeping sanctions against Russia, including bans on the import of Russian coal since August 2022, seaborne crude oil since December 2022 and petroleum products since February 2023.

Despite these efforts, Europe's energy decoupling from Russia was a consequence less of deliberate EU actions than of decisions made by the Kremlin. Moscow had already started to squeeze the EU gas market in 2021 by failing to fill Gazprom-owned storage sites within EU borders and restricting exports to only contracted volumes from the fourth quarter. Throughout 2022, Russia went further by demanding ruble-for-gas payments and later suspending gas shipments through the Nord Stream 1 pipeline, causing Europe's pipeline imports of natural gas from Russia to plummet by more than 80% between February and November 2022.[3]

The weaponisation of energy

This energy break-up is all the more remarkable given that the energy links were established during the Cold War and persisted for decades despite the existence of the Iron Curtain. The Soviet–European energy rapprochement was driven by the forces of geography and markets. Soviet and later Russian gas was abundant, nearby and cheap. Yet East–West energy infrastructure, especially long-distance gas pipelines from Siberia to Western Europe, was also built on political ideas about energy interdependence as a means of promoting peace and stability in world politics. Today, these assumptions have been marginalised. Energy interdependence is no longer seen as a bridge to overcome geopolitical difficulties but rather as a potential source of strategic vulnerability.

The war in Ukraine also marks a new era in the use of energy as a geopolitical weapon. For one, while Russia has a long history of using energy as a coercive tool, the blatancy and severity of its actions in 2022 against what was then its main gas customer, Germany, are unprecedented. For another, although the West has imposed energy sanctions on countries such as Iran, Iraq and Venezuela before, the sanctions and embargoes on Russia in response to the invasion of Ukraine are unmatched in scope, scale and impact. Moreover, the phrase "weaponising energy" has taken on a new meaning in the wake of Russian

---

3   See https://gasdashboard.entsog.eu/.

attacks on Ukraine's critical electricity infrastructure and the sabotage of the Nord Stream pipelines. This highlights the importance of security for critical infrastructure and vital nodes in the global energy network. Preserving energy security is no longer just a matter of making markets work, but increasingly a question entangled in broader issues of hard, (inter)national security.

Immediate winners and losers

On the eve of the full-scale invasion, Russia was by far the world's largest oil and gas exporter.[4] With its image as a reliable energy supplier in tatters, Russia is unlikely to reemerge as a major fossil fuel exporter to Europe. It has also lost its chance to maintain commercial energy ties even as Europe transitions to net zero – for instance, by exporting low-carbon hydrogen to the EU. Moreover, shifting Russia's energy exports eastward to compensate for the loss of its biggest market is no easy feat, given that such a pivot would require significant investment in new infrastructure. Consequently, it seems that the days of Russia as an energy superpower are ebbing away. Moscow will not regain its past clout.

Parallel to the energy decoupling between the West and Russia, the war in Ukraine has also spawned new energy trade links and created winners in the global energy market. Fossil fuel producers raked in a huge $2 billion windfall in 2022 above their 2021 net income.[5] One clear winner is Norway, which has seen windfall profits from increased demand for its natural gas in Europe as a result of Russia's gas cut-offs. Another significant winner is the United States, which has become the world's largest exporter of liquefied natural gas (LNG), overtaking Qatar in 2022. The EU now imports more LNG from the US than pipeline gas from Russia. US exports of crude oil and petroleum products have equally surged, reaching a record high in 2022.[6] Geopolitical considerations and sanctions rather than market logic underpin much of the ongoing rerouting of oil and gas trade flows.

---

4   Birol, F. (2023) "Where things stand in the global energy crisis one year on". IEA website, 23 February (https://www.iea.org/commentaries/where-things-stand-in-the-global-energy-crisis-one-year-on).
5   IEA (2022) "World energy outlook 2022", p. 19.
6   "US crude oil exports hit record high in 2022, EIA data shows". *Reuters*, 15 March 2023.

Setbacks in the Global South

The war between Russia and Ukraine has had significant energy implications beyond Europe, particularly for developing countries.[7] Europe's dash for LNG has exacerbated energy shortages and blackouts in countries such as Pakistan and Bangladesh. High oil and LNG prices have resuscitated some developing countries' demand for coal, a major contributor to air pollution and climate change. Inflation and rising interest rates, in turn, are limiting the ability of these countries to finance their own transitions towards cleaner energy sources, leaving them stuck in a fossil-fuel-dependent cycle.

Moreover, in 2022 the International Energy Agency (IEA) noted a fallback in global improvements in energy access for the first time in a long period, adding to the challenges faced by developing countries. While the IEA has long been tracking progress towards universal energy access, the Covid-19 pandemic and the global energy crunch of 2022 have now pushed that goal further out of reach.[8]

An accelerated energy transition

Despite such setbacks, the war has also spurred the acceleration of the global energy transition. This shift was already gaining momentum before the conflict, but it has since been put on steroids, with countries across the world now prioritising the adoption of clean energy sources as a matter of national security and energy sovereignty, instead of just for climate reasons.[9] In 2022, for the first time, energy-transition investment was on a par with fossil fuel investment.[10]

---

7   Ramachandran, V., and Kincer, J. (2023) "Europe's hunger for gas leaves poor countries high and dry". *Foreign Policy*, 1 February.

8   IEA (2022) "World energy outlook 2022".

9   Liebreich, M. (2022) "After Ukraine: the great clean energy acceleration". BloombergNEF, 30 September (https://about.bnef.com/blog/after-ukraine-the-great-clean-energy-acceleration/).

10   "Energy transition investment now on par with fossil fuel". BloombergNEF, 10 February 2023 (https://about.bnef.com/blog/energy-transition-investment-now-on-par-with-fossil-fuel/).

For instance, in Europe the deployment of heat pumps is surging (growing by more than 30% annually),[11] and there has been a significant increase in Europe's import of solar photovoltaic (PV) panels and modules from China (growing by 112% in 2022 compared with 2021).[12] The world is set to add 440 gigawatts of renewable power capacity in 2023, a huge jump from the previous year and more than double what it added in 2019.[13] The acceleration of the energy transition towards cleaner sources of energy has also led to a renewed focus on increased energy efficiency, with more buildings being renovated for this purpose.[14] The war might just be the catalyst the world needs to break its carbon addiction.

The return of the state

The war in Ukraine has also led to a resurgence of state intervention in energy matters and of industrial policy writ large. These trends were already visible prewar but have since accelerated.[15] Governments across the globe are now intervening in energy markets to shield consumers from high energy prices and to rescue energy companies from bankruptcy. For instance, the German government has taken steps to rescue energy company Uniper. Furthermore, there is now increased scrutiny of foreign investments in the energy sector. Governments are increasingly wary of foreign entities gaining control of critical energy infrastructure. This marks a departure from the old adage of leaving the market to operate freely. The state's return to energy matters is another reflection of the growing realisation that energy security is a vital component of national security.

---

11   Kurmayer, N. J. (2023) "Three countries became heat pump forerunners in 2022, Germany did not". *Euractiv*, 20 February (https://www.euractiv.com/section/energy-environment/news/three-countries-became-heat-pump-forerunners-in-2022-germany-did-not/).

12   Chen, R. (2023) "China's module exports hit high in 2022". Infolink Consulting website, 3 February (https://www.infolink-group.com/energy-article/solar-topic-Chinas-module-exports-hit-high-in-2022).

13   IEA (2023) "Renewable energy market update". Report, Paris, OECD/IEA, June.

14   IEA (2022) "Energy efficiency 2022". Report, Paris, OECD/IEA, December.

15   Bordoff, J., and O'Sullivan, M. L. (2022) "The new energy order: how governments will transform energy markets". *Foreign Affairs,* 101(4): 131–144.

Shaping factors in energy geopolitics

The China factor

The geopolitical alignment and energy policies of key actors will have a significant impact on the long-term energy consequences of the war in Ukraine. China, in particular, is the most critical player due to its sheer size and influence on energy markets. In the short term, a crucial question for 2023 is whether China's loosening of its zero-Covid policy will result in a demand shock for oil and gas. Some analysts foresee an oil price spike later in the year,[16] while the IEA believes that a surge in China's appetite for LNG could hinder Europe's efforts to replenish its natural gas reserves during the summer, which is critical for a safe winter of 2023–2024.[17]

China, together with India and other emerging economies in Asia, is also a critical actor when it comes to the effectiveness of Western oil sanctions against Russia. While Europe, the US and the UK have imposed unilateral embargoes on the bulk of Russian oil imports, the G7 countries have also introduced a price cap on Russian oil exports.[18] However, non-Western countries are increasing their oil imports from Russia. Since late 2022, Russia has become both India's and China's top oil supplier.[19] While Urals oil, the country's main crude export blend, has been trading at prices well below the $60-a-barrel price cap and the average price of Brent (the international benchmark), by April 2023 the weighted average price for Russian crude exports had risen above the cap.[20] This is due to the fact that the key buyers of Russian oil are not abiding by the price cap.[21]

---

16 Slav, I. (2023) "Oil prices are set to rise throughout 2023". Oilprice.com, 7 March.

17 IEA (2022) "How to avoid gas shortages in the European Union in 2023". Report, Paris, OECD/IEA, December.

18 The price cap aims to diminish Russia's oil export revenues and hinder its ability to finance its war efforts in Ukraine while keeping the global economy stable by ensuring sufficient oil supplies. The G7 is leveraging the dominant position of Western oil tanker insurance and reinsurance firms to impose such a price cap.

19 Cang, A. (2023) "Russia jumps above Saudi Arabia as China's biggest oil supplier", *Bloomberg*, 23 March; Sharma, R. (2023) "India's imports of Russian oil dwarf Iraq, Saudi flows", *Bloomberg*, 2 May.

20 Wilson, T. (2023) "G7 claims success with price cap that keeps Russian oil flowing". *Financial Times*, 10 May.

21 "India and China snap up Russian oil in April above price cap". *Reuters*, 18 April 2023.

Middle East: new allegiances?

With Russia redirecting its energy exports to Asia, and Europe turning to the US, the postinvasion energy map increasingly reflects geopolitical fault lines. However, the energy-rich Gulf countries are defying Western pressure to break with Russia – a fellow OPEC+[22] producer – over its invasion of Ukraine. In fact, since October 2022, OPEC+ has agreed on three oil production cuts, defying warnings from the IEA that such cuts risk fuelling inflation and harming the global economy.[23] These moves show that Washington's influence in the region is waning, partly as a result of its own strategic retreat from the Middle East in the wake of the shale revolution.

Saudi Arabia and its Gulf allies have also ignored US pressure to reduce their dealings with China. China is now the biggest oil customer of the Middle East and has gained geopolitical influence in the region, as illustrated by its recent success in brokering diplomatic talks between archrivals Iran and Saudi Arabia. Chinese investments in the Middle East through the Belt and Road Initiative are also soaring, with Saudi Arabia emerging as the second-largest recipient in 2022.[24] Conversely, Saudi Aramco has recently made a series of investments in the refining industries of China, India, South Korea and Malaysia.[25] In November 2022 China and Qatar agreed to a $60 billion, 27-year LNG contract.[26]

These trends illustrate that Russia will face tough competition from the Middle East if it wants to pivot its oil and gas sales to Asia. They also show that Europe will face tough competition from Asia if it wants to secure access to oil and gas from the Persian Gulf. Europe's energy dependence on the Middle East and North Africa has already grown following its turn away from Russia, creating new supply risks and curbing

---

22 OPEC+ refers to a broad coalition of oil producers, including all thirteen members of the Organization of the Petroleum Exporting Countries as well as a host of non-OPEC countries such as Russia, Mexico and Kazakhstan.
23 Horner, W. (2023) "Saudi-led oil cuts risk fueling inflation and harming global economy, IEA says". *Wall Street Journal*, 14 April.
24 Nedopil, C. (2023) "China Belt and Road Initiative (BRI) investment report 2022". Green Finance and Development Center, January (https://greenfdc.org/china-belt-and-road-initiative-bri-investment-report-2022/).
25 Wilson, T. (2023) "Saudi Aramco strengthens China ties with two refinery deals". *Financial Times*, 27 March.
26 Dargin, J. (2022) "What's at stake in the massive China–Qatar gas deal". Carnegie Endowment for International Peace website, 29 December (https://carnegieendowment.org/2022/12/29/what-s-at-stake-in-massive-china-qatar-gas-deal-pub-88696).

Europe's political room for manoeuvre vis-à-vis major regional energy exporters such as Qatar, Azerbaijan and Algeria. It should be clear by now that the costs of the EU's import dependence on fossil fuels are not just economic, but also geopolitical.

Energy security during the transition

A key lesson driven home by the war in Ukraine and the global energy crisis is that energy security remains a significant concern for many countries, despite the ongoing shift towards renewable sources in the global energy mix. Prior to the conflict, EU leaders may have grown somewhat complacent, assuming that the European Green Deal and the quest for carbon neutrality would automatically mitigate future oil and gas price spikes and supply disruptions. The war has made it abundantly clear that the transition away from oil and gas will be more of a bumpy road than a smooth one, and that the uninterrupted availability of fossil fuels during the transition is of pivotal importance to ensuring that the lights and the heating stay on.

As global oil demand peaks and starts to decline, the world may become increasingly reliant on low-cost producers. In fact, the IEA estimates that OPEC's market share might actually increase under a net-zero scenario, from 35% today to 52% in 2050.[27] Recent investment decisions made by Saudi Aramco to increase its production capacity clearly demonstrate the country's ambition to remain the "last producer standing".[28] These trends and events underscore the need for continued vigilance over the security of supply of traditional fuels even in a world heading for net-zero emissions.

Hydrogen import security

At the same time, the very notion of energy security is evolving alongside shifts in the global energy mix. While many countries will become less energy-import dependent, and therefore less beholden to their geopolitical adversaries, new dependencies will arise. For instance, the EU has bet heavily on hydrogen as a tool to achieve climate neutrality and reduce reliance on Russian gas. More specifically, the EU aims for 20 million tonnes of renewable hydrogen consumption by 2030, which is around 5% of

---

27   IEA (2022) "World energy outlook 2022", p. 329.
28   Wilson, T. (2023) "Saudi Aramco bets on being the last oil major standing". *Financial Times*, 12 January.

expected total EU primary energy.[29] Half of that would be domestically produced, and the other half would be imported, either in pure form (H_2) or as hydrogen-based derivatives such as ammonia (NH_3).

However, importing green hydrogen will not necessarily reproduce the vulnerabilities linked to importing natural gas. Unlike oil and gas, these green molecules are manufactured products, providing Europe with more opportunities to choose its trading partners. Countries such as Namibia, Chile and Morocco have the potential to become exporters of green fuels. Global low-carbon hydrogen exports could reach 12 million tonnes by 2030, coming from a geographically diverse set of countries.[30] While importing hydrogen through refurbished natural gas pipelines is by far the cheapest option for bulk volumes, Europe should learn from its current gas crisis and avoid repeating old patterns of dependence and vulnerability.[31]

Supply chain resilience

Since the Covid-19 pandemic, clean energy supply chains have faced multiple disruptions, resulting in higher prices for wind and batteries.[32] Europe – with its heavy reliance on imported raw materials (such as lithium, cobalt, nickel and rare earths), components (including solar wafers and cells) and manufactured goods (like batteries, electrolysers and heat pumps) – is particularly vulnerable to supply chain shocks.[33] It is especially dependent on China for the supply of energy-transition minerals, components and goods.[34]

In February 2023, the EU Commission presented a series of policy proposals under the Green Deal Industrial Plan, aimed at relocating vital supply chains to within Europe. The policy package's focal points include the Critical Raw Materials Act, which establishes targets for domestic mining, refining and recycling of raw materials by 2030, and the Net-Zero

---

29   Bond, K., and Butler-Sloss, S. (2022) "The energy transition in Europe: the shape of things to come". Report, Rocky Mountains Institute, October (https://rmi.org/insight/energy-transition-in-europe/).

30   IEA (2022) "Global hydrogen review 2022". Report, Paris, OECD/IEA, September.

31   IRENA (2022) *The Geopolitics of the Energy Transformation: The Hydrogen Factor* (Abu Dhabi: International Renewable Energy Agency).

32   Energy Transitions Commission (2023) "Better, faster, cleaner: securing clean energy technology supply chains". Report, London, June.

33   Energy Transitions Commission (2023) "EU policy toolkit". Report, London, June.

34   European Commission (2023) "Study on the critical raw materials for the EU 2023: final report". Brussels, 16 March.

Industry Act, which sets the headline goal of ensuring domestic manufacturing caters to at least 40% of the EU's annual deployment needs by 2030.[35] The plan is also a response to the United States' efforts to promote domestic clean energy manufacturing through measures such as the Inflation Reduction Act, passed in August 2022.

However, it is important to distinguish between dependence on oil and gas imports on the one hand and import reliance for raw materials, components and manufactured goods on the other. Disruptions in oil or gas supplies have immediate and far-reaching consequences for energy security and the overall economy. In contrast, disruptions in the supply of raw materials, components or manufactured goods affect in particular the manufacturing or deployment of clean energy technology.[36] Furthermore, unlike with fossil fuels, there are more opportunities to reduce, reuse and recycle raw materials, as well as to reshore the manufacturing of clean energy technologies. The EU's proposed Critical Raw Materials Act, for example, aims to source at least 15% of its annual consumption of strategic raw materials from recycling by 2030.

Physical resilience to climate change

Another way in which the traditional notion of energy security needs updating is by incorporating its physical resilience to the effects of climate change. The global energy crunch of 2022, for example, was influenced by changed weather patterns related to climate change. In Europe, reduced rainfall constrained hydropower capacity in Norway, and an extended heatwave and drought in the summer affected the supply of coal to the German industrial heartland by bringing bulk shipping through the Rhine to a standstill.

More such knock-on effects can be expected as the number of heatwaves, floodings and hurricanes increases. Some parts of our energy infrastructure are particularly vulnerable. It is estimated that a quarter of today's refineries are exposed to the risk of destructive cyclones, and around one-third of refineries are threatened by sea-level rise and storm surges. At the same time, climate change will affect energy demand

---

35 European Commission (2023) "The Green Deal Industrial Plan: putting Europe's net-zero industry in the lead". Press release, Brussels, 1 February.
36 IRENA (2023) *The Geopolitics of the Energy Transformation.*

patterns, raising the need for cooling during heatwaves and thereby adding strain to electricity grids during peak hours.[37]

Rerouting flows amid an uncertain transition

There is no way back to business as usual in energy relations between the EU and Russia. Even if the war finished tomorrow, trust has been broken and the Nord Stream pipelines, which were damaged by unexplained blasts in September 2022, would require very costly repairs before they could be used again. A resumption of Gazprom's large-scale pipeline deliveries to Europe would also require a drastic change in the policy stance of both sides (in other words, the lifting of sanctions) and a solution to the arbitration cases that some European companies have filed against Gazprom over missing gas deliveries.[38]

Some argue that Russian gas should not be written off too soon.[39] While the EU has banned oil imports from Russia, it has not done the same with natural gas, even though such a proposal was discussed in the margins of a G7 meeting in May 2023.[40] Russian gas still flows into Europe via pipelines through Ukraine and Turkey, and, increasingly, also via LNG ships and terminals. It is not entirely unthinkable that European fears of deindustrialisation and an acute need for cash in the Kremlin would lead to the restoration of some of the lost gas trade flows if Russia reversed its aggression of Ukraine. Russian gas transit through Ukraine is also one of the quickest ways to raise Kyiv's hard currency earnings, which could pay for the country's reconstruction after the war, yet the current gas transit contract expires at the end of 2024 and its prolongation is highly unlikely.[41] There is no doubt that Europe will never return to the same level of import dependence on Russia as before the war.

---

37   IEA (2022) "Climate resilience for energy security". Report, Paris, OECD/IEA, November.

38   Chi, K. C., Corbeau, A.-S., Joseph, I., and Mitrova, T. (2023) "Future options for Russian gas exports". Report, Columbia Center on Global Energy Policy, 19 January (https://www.energypolicy.columbia.edu/publications/future-options-russian-gas-exports/).

39   Blas, J. (2022) "Can Europe's energy bridge to Russia ever be rebuilt?" *Bloomberg*, 12 December.

40   Gavin, G., and Jack, V. (2023) "Europe balks at adding Russian gas pipeline ban to sanctions package". *Politico*, 16 May.

41   Corbeau, A.-S., and Mitrova, T. (2023) "Will the Ukrainian gas transit contract continue beyond 2024?" Blog post, Columbia Center on Global Energy Policy, 8 June (https://www.energypolicy.columbia.edu/will-the-ukrainian-gas-transit-contract-continue-beyond-2024/).

Russia will attempt to pivot its gas exports eastward. Russia supplied just over 10 billion cubic meters (bcm) of pipeline gas to Asia in 2021, compared with 155 bcm of pipeline gas exports to the EU. In 2022, pipeline flows to Europe fell to 85 bcm, while flows to Asia rose to 15 bcm.[42] In a best-case scenario for Russia, it will take at least a decade to scale up its gas exports to Asia to match the prewar export levels to Europe.[43] Moscow will also attempt to find new buyers for its oil, either through official sales or clandestine deals. Russia has reportedly amassed a "shadow fleet" of oil tankers to skirt Western sanctions.[44] Nonetheless, the IEA projects that Russian fossil fuel exports will never recover to the levels of 2021 and the country's share of global oil and gas trade will fall by half by 2030.[45]

Like the ongoing technological decoupling between China and the US, the fragmentation of the energy relationship between Russia and Europe underscores the growing tendency of bloc formation in the global economy. Most of Russia's prewar oil exports went to NATO members, and sanctions are now pushing Moscow to find new buyers. This marks the end of three decades of a globally integrated oil market and heralds a new period of a what Daniel Yergin calls a "partitioned" oil market.[46] However, the emerging energy blocs do not fit into a simple autocracy–democracy dichotomy. The Middle Eastern nations will play a vital role as exporters to both Europe and Asia. Furthermore, it is probable that shipments of LNG from Australia and the United States to China will continue in the foreseeable future.[47]

One of the key risks of bloc-forming is that the needs and voices of smaller or less powerful countries are left behind. New geopolitical ties may be drawn between the energy-hungry Global South and authoritarian petroleum exporters keen to find new markets. In this era of energy

---

42 "With much of the European market lost, Gazprom looks closer to home". *Insight Blog*, S&P Global Commodity Insights, 24 February 2023 (www.spglobal.com/commodityinsights/en/market-insights/blogs/natural-gas/022423-russia-ukraine-gazprom-european-market).

43 Bois von Kursk, O., et al. (2022) "Navigating energy transitions: mapping the road to 1.5 °C". Report, International Institute for Sustainable Development, 21 October.

44 Sheppard, D., Cook, C., and Ivanova, P. (2022) "Russia assembles 'shadow fleet' of tankers to help blunt oil sanctions". *Financial Times*, 2 December.

45 IEA (2022) "World energy outlook 2022", p. 24.

46 Yergin, D. (2022) "Putin can't count on the global oil market". *Wall Street Journal*, 26 December.

47 Bunde, T., Eisentraut, S., Knapp, N., et al. (2023) "Munich security report 2023: Re:vision". Munich Security Conference, February.

nationalism – where major economic blocs are striving for technological sovereignty through rewiring supply chains – developing countries are often forced to serve as mere raw material suppliers.

Russia's war has resulted in a global "dash for gas", a rush to build out new fossil gas infrastructure around the world, and particularly in Africa, to replace Russian supplies in Europe.[48] This ranges from revived plans for a trans-Saharan gas pipeline from Nigeria to Algeria, to the proposal of new LNG import facilities in Europe, to renewed momentum to develop and expand LNG terminals in Congo, Mauritania and Senegal. Developing new infrastructure for natural gas and other fossil fuels carries the risk of locking in carbon-intensive assets and dependencies for many decades, further decreasing the likelihood that global warming could be contained below 1.5 °C.[49] At the same time, new fossil energy investments may face higher risks of stranded assets if climate policy is strengthened.

The concept of stranded assets has geopolitical relevance. Modelling typically foresees that high-cost producers will be the first to be kicked out of the market.[50] Judging by recent trends, however, it is more likely that geopolitics will dictate whose oil and gas stays in the ground, rather than the position of various producer countries along the cost curve. While US oil sanctions against Venezuela, Iran and Russia come with distinct political rationales, the corollary is that they help to cement the US's position as the world's biggest oil producer by keeping "hostile oil" in the ground.[51] The fight over whose oil stays in the ground is fought in many different ways.

The production cuts announced by OPEC+ since the end of 2022, for instance, can be interpreted as a way to seize back control of the oil market. Parallel to the gas war between Russia and the EU, a broader oil war has emerged between Saudi Arabia and the US.[52] Throughout 2022 the oil market was balanced by the largest release from Western strategic oil reserves in history. The effort was spearheaded by the US, which alone

---

48 "Analysis: dash for gas in response to Russia/Ukraine crisis could lock in warming". Press release, Climate Action Tracker, 8 June 2022 (https://climateactiontracker.org/press/analysis-response-to-russia-ukraine-crisis-could-lock-in-warming/).

49 Bois von Kursk, O., et al. (2022) "Navigating energy transitions".

50 See, for example, McGlade, C., and Ekins, P. (2015) "The geographical distribution of fossil fuels unused when limiting global warming to 2 °C". *Nature*, 517(7533): 187–190.

51 Verbruggen, A., and Van de Graaf, T. (2013) "Peak oil supply or oil not for sale?" *Futures*, 53: 74–85.

52 Van de Graaf, T. (2022) "A storm is brewing in oil markets after the OPEC+ cuts". *Democracy in Exile*, 2 November.

released some 180 million barrels of crude. The Saudi energy minister criticised the move as an attempt "to manipulate [oil] markets".[53] The G7 price cap on Russian oil similarly frustrated many OPEC governments, which fear the measure could be used against them in the future.[54] Yet Middle Eastern producers have the upper hand in the medium and long term, as the golden age of US shale oil production is drawing to a close.[55]

Looking forward, we can expect more volatility in oil and gas markets and a concomitant oscillation of fossil energy prices. As for European gas, futures markets expect neither a return to the extreme gas price levels of 2022 nor a return to the price levels of the 2010s. Uncertainty is clouding oil and gas demand projections and holding back investment in oil and gas exploration.[56] While this lack of upstream spending is actually in line with what is needed in net-zero scenarios, supply risks loom large if investment in alternative energy technologies does not follow suit on an adequate scale.

Countries and regions are implementing policies to shape global supply chains by reshoring, nearshoring and friendshoring to become less dependent on geopolitical adversaries. There is a growing recognition of the risks associated with the concentration of critical mineral supply chains and the need to reduce the risk of technology dependence. However, given the long lead times in developing new mines and processing and manufacturing facilities, the EU's high dependence on China for critical materials will remain a fact of life for at least a decade. Nonetheless, diversification policies will be a defining trend shaping the future of energy geopolitics.

Policy implications for the EU

Despite triumphant messages that Putin "overplayed his hand" and that Europe has "won the energy battle", the EU should not be complacent.[57]

---

53 El Wardany, S., Fattah, Z., and Smith, G. (2022) "Saudi energy minister warns against depleting crude buffers". *Bloomberg*, 25 October.

54 Brower, D., Sheppard, D., England, A., and Schwartz, F. (2022) "The new oil war: Opec moves against the US". *Financial Times*, 7 October.

55 Brower, D., and McCormick, M. (2023) "What the end of the US shale revolution would mean for the world". *Financial Times*, 16 January.

56 Blas, J. (2022) "We told Big Oil not to invest. Don't complain now". *Bloomberg*, 2 November.

57 Van de Graaf, T. (2022) "Europe's energy crunch: no time for complacency". GIES Occasional Paper, December (https://www.ugent.be/ps/politiekewetenschappen/gies/en/research/publications/gies_papers/2023-global-energy-crisis/europes-energy-crunch-no-time-for-complacency).

Europe's surging LNG imports, which allowed it to replenish its gas inventories for the winter, have come at a very high cost of approximately €50 billion in 2022, ten times the historical average.[58] The import bill will likely remain elevated for years to come, and Bloomberg has calculated that surging energy costs have already saddled the EU economy with a bill of roughly $1 trillion.[59]

Moreover, in some cases the EU has freed itself from its energy dependence on Russia only by turning to other suppliers, some of which display a poor track record in terms of human rights, geopolitical stability or democracy. Therefore, rather than just shifting from one problematic supplier to another, the EU should continue to double down on its plans to phase out fossil fuel consumption altogether and prioritise the development of green technologies.

As energy trade flows are rerouted, the EU faces a challenging balancing act between economic efficiency and geopolitical resilience in building out the supply chains for green and digital technologies. At the centre of the EU's approach is the vague notion of "strategic autonomy". While the EU should avoid repeating past mistakes, particularly its overdependence on Russian gas, it should strive to preserve global markets, trade and investment flows. Some major economies, including the United States, are enacting protectionist and trade-distorting measures. In contrast to the resource-rich US, however, the EU will continue to remain heavily dependent on imports of energy, including green hydrogen and raw materials.

Given that the EU will remain entangled in global energy interdependencies, it should invest heavily in energy diplomacy efforts aimed at ensuring sustainable, responsible and reliable supply chains for its Green Deal. This includes setting priorities for green investment abroad, through the Global Gateway and otherwise. Investments in Africa should be stepped up in a way that not just benefits the EU's needs for imports of raw materials and green hydrogen but also allows African economies to climb up the value chain, improve their long-term economic outlooks and advance their own energy transition.

Another promising idea is for the EU to use its market power to jointly purchase energy. This approach has been successful in vaccine

---

58   Sharafedin, B. (2022) "European gas storage on track to meet target but at a cost". *Reuters*, 4 August (https://www.reuters.com/business/energy/european-gas-storage-track-meet-target-cost-2022-08-04/).

59   "Europe's $1 trillion energy bill only marks start of the crisis". *Bloomberg*, 18 December 2022.

procurement and is now being extended to natural gas, hydrogen and critical raw materials. Joint purchasing pools the member states' market power, allowing the EU to set the terms of trade and import hydrogen through euro-denominated deals. It also enables Europe to avoid locking in too many supplies through long-term contracts, especially in the case of LNG.

By pursuing strategic autonomy without jeopardising open trade and investment frameworks, and by investing in green and digital technologies both at home and abroad, the EU can create a more sustainable and resilient energy future for itself and its global partners while maintaining its role as a major player in global energy geopolitics.

Thomas Pellerin-Carlin

3 | Overcoming the great fossil fuel shock: building an energy system that serves a free, secure and green Europe

Fossil fuel crises are intrinsically linked to the European choice for an energy system dependent on imported fossil fuels. This choice was made by Western European states after World War II, even as the process of decolonisation limited the European Unions' influence on oil and gas producing territories. This created the conditions for the first two oil shocks, in 1973 and 1979, which severely damaged member states' economic model. The choice for dependence on imported fossil fuels was tacitly confirmed even after the fall of the Soviet Union, with newer EU member states continuing to rely on Soviet-era infrastructure to import Russian coal, oil and gas to the EU. This, in turn, created the conditions for the first three Russian gas crises, in 2006, 2009 and 2014. It also did not protect Europe from the severe economic impact of the 2008 oil shock, which played a role in triggering the Great Recession of 2009.

From this historical perspective, the 2021–2023 fossil fuel shock is not a surprise. When Gazprom chose to limit its gas supplies to the EU as early as the summer of 2021, the EU gas price increased sharply, before skyrocketing in December 2021. When Russia then chose to launch the full-scale invasion of Ukraine on 24 February 2022, it caught gas markets by surprise. In April 2022, as the Russian army was defeated by Ukrainian forces in the north of Ukraine, Putin shifted gear to a protracted war, and further weaponised the EU's dependence on Russian gas by cutting all pipeline Russian gas supplies to several EU member states, including Bulgaria, Poland, Finland and Denmark. Meanwhile, global oil prices were rising from their low Covid-19 lockdown levels, even if they remained well below the 2012–2014 average.

The 2021–2022 shock: pushing the EU energy system into a new era

Following several disruptions in the past, what makes the 2021–2023 great fossil fuel shock special is not the crisis itself, but its degree and its long-lasting consequences.

In terms of degree, previous crises tended to focus either on oil or on gas, while the 2021 shock impacted both, and occurred at a moment when global coal prices were high due to global post-Covid economic recovery and electricity prices were high due to a sudden drop in production of the French nuclear fleet, because of safety concerns, and of EU hydropower systems, because of droughts. It was therefore a nearly perfect storm.

In terms of duration, while the first three gas crises and the 2008 oil shock were intense, they had a short duration, with both prices and material supply returning quickly to normal levels. The situation that started in 2021 bears a closer resemblance to the first oil shock: not a short-term crisis, but the abrupt entry into a new era. For Western Europe, the 1973 oil shock ended the era of reliable supply of cheap oil from the Middle East. Similarly, the 2021 gas shock, amplified by the invasion of Ukraine, likely ended the era of reliable supply of cheap gas from Russia to the EU. The evolution of the price of oil and gas matters for the EU economy, since about two thirds of the EU's energy comes from oil (38%) and gas (28%),[1] with oil being the key energy source for transportation, while gas has a more polyvalent role, as it is used for heating buildings, industrial processes and electricity generation.

As the energy system of today has been shaped by decades of previous policy and private investment decisions, even a crisis as severe as the one Europe has been facing since 2021 falls short of drastically reshaping the EU energy system in the short term. Among the many elements of continuity, three stand out.

First is the persistence of fossil fuels in the EU energy mix. Even if the 2021–2023 high fossil gas prices and fears of a gas shortage limited demand for gas, the demand for oil remained largely stable, while coal consumption slightly increased. Consolidated data for 2022 remain to be published, but evidence suggests that the change in gas consumption between 2021 and 2022, while significant, is likely to remain of a similar order of magnitude to the type of changes that come with an economic

---

1 Data are for the year 2019; see BP (2022) "Statistical review of world energy", June.

recession or a very mild winter (for example, EU gas demand fell by 11% between 2013 and 2014, mostly because of a very mild winter that led Europeans to require less gas for heating and electricity). There are, however, elements of discontinuity, as the politics and economics of fossil gas drastically shifted in the EU.

Second, the EU gas and electricity security system remains resilient. Even at the worst moment of the winter of 2022–2023, the EU managed to avoid gas and electricity shortages. This remarkable resilience was first and foremost due to the existence of the EU gas and electricity market, which had sufficient interconnections, market integration and governmental cooperation to ensure that the gas molecules and electrons would flow to where they were needed most. To oversimplify, both the German gas system and the French electricity system were bailed out by Europe. This technical, economic and political resilience will, however, be further tested by the winter of 2023–2024, which may be especially difficult if the droughts worsen in the EU or in other countries dependent on liquefied natural gas (LNG), if the summer is especially hot or the winter especially cold, or if the global LNG market tightens as a result of the end of the Chinese zero-Covid policy or other drivers.

Third, the ramp-up of renewables remains slow. Even with renewable energy being rightly described as "freedom energy" by German Finance Minister Christian Lindner at the beginning of Russia's full-scale invasion of Ukraine, renewable energy installation, especially for wind power, continued its progression at a limited speed. Consolidated EU-27 numbers for 2022 are not available at the moment of writing, but Germany plays a major role as by far the biggest producer of renewable electricity in the Union. One potential element of disruption would be if a wider number of policymakers supported bold renewable policies for the sake of ensuring energy security. In terms of public policy, this would make sense, since foreign autocrats who are in the midst of an invasion can cut off oil or gas supply to the EU but remain unable to stop the sun from shining or the wind from blowing. With the war came a newfound sense of urgency to deploy renewable energy sources, leading to the rapid adoption of emergency regulations at the EU and national levels to speed up the deployment of renewables in Europe in the short term (2023–2024) and medium term (2030). This reinforces the preexisting renewable agenda, but the extent of the change remains unclear.

Alongside these factors of relative continuity, the war in Ukraine has triggered three discontinuities that are reshaping the EU's energy policy landscape. For one, the politics of fossil gas have shifted on their head.

During the last two decades, both gas lobbyists and EU and international institutions were praising fossil gas, presenting it as "*natural* gas", the "cleanest fossil fuel" that would play a role as a cheap "transition fuel". In other words, gas as the lesser of many other evils, especially coal. But now EU dependence on Russian fossil gas is public enemy number one. This new anti-Russian-gas focus is likely to persist for years – if not decades – to come and will weaken the pro-gas coalition in Brussels and national capitals.

Another discontinuity is that the economics of gas have drastically changed. Thanks to cheap Russian gas, a lot of EU companies from Germany and the rest of the continent could improve their cost competitiveness in the global market relative to those paying higher prices for LNG, such as their Japanese, Korean or Chinese competitors. But the EU gas price will now likely remain closely tied to the global LNG price, levelling the global playing field to the disfavour of EU companies – and households. In contrast, this increases the economic incentive to cut gas consumption, whether through rationing (for example, temporary shutdowns of industrial facilities, especially during gas price spikes in the winter), energy efficiency or switching towards other energy sources (such as coal, oil or renewables).

As gas economics were challenged, virtually all the governments of the EU member states reacted by launching vast subsidy schemes, which corresponds to a third dimension of discontinuity induced by the war in Ukraine. According to Bruegel, around €600 billion of public money was mobilised between September 2021 and September 2022 to curb the effects of the fossil fuel shock.[2] Virtually none of that money went directly to subsidising the green transformation. A lot was spent in the form of cheques for households, while much of the rest went to fossil fuel subsidies. The €600 billion headline figure makes this fossil fuel subsidy campaign one of the most important – if not the single most important – in European history. Ironically, part of those subsidies were funded by special taxes or claw-back systems targeting profits from renewable electricity generators. In other words, this policy used clean-energy money to subsidise fossil fuels – precisely the opposite of those member states' past promises to phase out fossil fuel subsidies in order to fund the green transition.

---

2 Sgaravatti, G., Tagliapietra, S., Trasi, C., et al. (2021) "National policies to shield consumers from rising energy prices". Bruegel Datasets, first published 4 November 2021, last consulted 1 May 2023 (https://www.bruegel.org/dataset/national-policies-shield-consumers-rising-energy-prices).

Key variables shaping the EU energy transition

Beyond those elements of continuity and discontinuity, there are several key variables whose evolution is uncertain and will significantly alter Europe's energy course.

To begin with, the speed and scale of the renewable energy scale-up will be crucial. The structurally higher and more uncertain price of fossil gas creates a renewed economic incentive to scale up the production of renewable electricity and renewable heat. Achieving the EU renewable energy target for 2030[3] will require a massive ramp-up that should be two to three times bigger than what the EU has seen in the last 15 years. The relative success or failure of such a speedy development of renewables in the coming years will be key to Europe's energy security, energy affordability and climate action.

The cost of capital is another key factor in the green transformation. Most clean-economy projects require much higher capital expenditure (CAPEX) (for example, the investment required to renovate a home and buy a heat pump to heat it) but also much less operational expenditure (OPEX) (which is near zero for a renovated home, and much lower when operating a heat pump than when buying gas to power a gas boiler). Conversely, most fossil fuel projects are OPEX-intensive (for example, over a 20-year period, most of the money spent by a household for gas heating is spent on buying gas, rather than buying the gas boiler). To sum up: the green transformation largely entails shifting from an OPEX-heavy economic model to a CAPEX-heavy one.[4] As capital cost is a key factor that drives CAPEX up, while having little to no impact on OPEX, its level will be a critical variable. The lower the capital cost, the faster and cheaper the transition.

Looking at political actors, one key variable remains the perceptions held by citizens, and citizens' political expression through demonstration, voting and other political actions. One of the drivers behind the policies of the European Green Deal was the important mobilisation of a part of the European youth, symbolised by Greta Thunberg and other teenagers and young adults in several member states. The magnitude and

---

3   In early 2023, the European Parliament and the Council of the European Union reached a compromise on the Renewable Energy Directive, enshrining the objective of ensuring that 42.5% of the EU's final energy consumption in 2030 comes from renewables. According to Eurostat data, that share increased from 9.6% in 2004 to 16% in 2012 and 21.8% in 2021.

4   There are, however, some exceptions, such as the production of green ammonia.

mode of operation of those movements will impact future policymakers. For instance, a comeback of the massive peaceful demonstrations of 2018 and 2019 may again increase the pressure on politicians to act and may help keep climate change high on the national and European political agendas. Conversely, the mediatisation of more extreme modes of operation – used by movements such as Extinction Rebellion – has less predictable outcomes. They do manage to keep climate high on the political agenda, but at the cost of using more divisive methods that can antagonise another segment of the population that can, in turn, become opponents of specific policies.

The beginning of a convergence of the EU climate community with the EU security and defence community would be another important dimension of change. Since 24 February 2022 it has become clear that virtually all climate policy measures, such as sufficiency transformations, public transportation, renewable energy installations and housing renovations, are also certain to advance EU geopolitical strategic interests, as they reduce the EU demand for – and therefore the global price of – Russian oil and gas.[5] Yet those two communities remain distant. However, an intensification of the contacts between the two communities, including the creation of dedicated platforms and think tanks modelled on the US example of SAFE (Securing America's Future Energy),[6] could help enrich the narrative for climate action with a national security narrative, both supporting the same types of public policy measures.

Finally, an intellectual factor to watch for will be the understanding of the extent to which energy sufficiency becomes a mainstream concept – if at all. Energy sufficiency is a concept defined by the Intergovernmental Panel on Climate Change as a set of policies and behaviours that deliver well-being while reducing the consumption of water, energy, land and raw materials to remain within planetary boundaries. It also proved to be a potentially useful concept for convincing EU citizens and businesses to change their behaviour in order to help their countries overcome the severe fossil fuel shock exacerbated by the Russian full-scale invasion of Ukraine. Typical sufficiency measures used since the start of the shock include choosing to wear warmer clothes at home in winter to ensure well-being even at 18 °C rather than 22 °C (which in turn delivers an energy saving of around 25% for that household), driving within voluntary lower

---

5   The only significant exception might be the short-term trade-off between gas and lignite as fuels for electricity generation, the former being a lesser evil from a climate perspective, while the latter delivers energy security at the cost of a major climate impact.

6   See https://secureenergy.org/about/.

speed limits on highways, and switching from hot to mild or cold water for specific parts of a building. Further studies are needed to assess the role that sufficiency behaviours played in reducing EU oil, gas and electricity consumption.[7]

Looking ahead: what scenarios are available for the EU energy transition in a post-2022 world?

The future of the EU energy system is uncertain. To inform policymakers on the key policy choices and options ahead, two brief scenarios, presenting drastically different futures, can be outlined. Both of them are internally coherent and based on the aforementioned variables. One aim of this exercise is to identify "no-regret options" that policymakers can undertake come what may.

Scenario 1: a subsidised fossil fuel stalemate

As the economic, climate and geopolitical hardship continues, no consensus emerges. Dissensus between member states and political families creates a political deadlock in Brussels. Liberals and conservatives turn against the Green Deal, blaming it for all of Europe's problems. The German government gives up on the hope of finding a joint European solution and goes on a national public subsidy spending spree that heavily disrupts the single market and creates a confidence breach between Germany and its traditional closest partners, such as the Netherlands and Sweden, who, in turn, debate starting a national subsidy spending spree of their own. With the end of NextGenerationEU in 2026, southern and eastern EU member states drastically cut climate investments to regain fiscal space that is then invested in the increase of oil and gas subsidies for their industry and households. In that context of European weakness, the far-right consolidates its power in Hungary and Italy, conquers the majority in France, Spain and Romania, and pressures both social democrats and Christian democrats to adopt a populist stance on climate change in Denmark, the Netherlands and Austria.

As global oil and gas prices stay at their 2023 level, member states pay hundreds of billions of euros every year in fossil fuel subsidies. To

---

[7] The research project CLEVER (https://clever-energy-scenario.eu/) is contributing to the analysis of energy sufficiency's potential as a new driver of the EU's energy and climate policy, but it is too soon to tell to what extent the 2021–2023 fossil fuel shock will be seen in retrospect as the beginning of a new era of sufficiency.

avoid an increase in the deficit, they adopt new, permanent taxation on the profits of renewable electricity developers, effectively taking money away from renewable energy companies and channelling it to fossil fuel. In a context of high concerns over public debt, member states' climate investments are frequently cut to limit annual deficits.

As the political commitment to the Green Deal dissipates, private investors shy away from investing in green projects in Europe and go to the US and China, where public support is generous. In Europe, capital costs for renewable energy and energy efficiency skyrocket, depriving most European businesses and families of access to the finance required to make profitable climate investments. Stuck between a rock and a hard place, EU wind power companies continue to lose money every year, and are finally bought by their American and Chinese competitors, mirroring the 2010s sale of Electricity of Portugal to a Chinese company and the sale of Alstom-Energie to an American one.

Energy sufficiency becomes a topic of culture war. In a swing to the extreme, a segment of the EU population takes pride in pollution, and some new polluting behaviours become trendy. Private jets are transformed into restaurants, flying to exclusive destinations just for "touch-and-go" meals. Meanwhile, a deep-ecology minority grows and engages in its own form of culture war. They slash the tires of all cars, while attacking vegetarian restaurants for serving dairy products. Overall, EU greenhouse gas emissions remain very high, and even increase in the transport and food sectors. The building and electricity sectors remain the only ones where greenhouse gas emissions decrease, but at a pace that is insufficient. On the global stage, Europe loses its climate credibility, and the anti-European campaigns centred on the vision of Europeans as global hypocrites gain traction.

Scenario 2: a green revolution

As the economic, climate and geopolitical hardship continues, a widespread consensus arises: investments in renewable energy, energy efficiency and energy sufficiency are vital to ensure the freedom of European nations.

In the 2024 EU elections, political families from across much of the European political spectrum agree on a wartime-like scale-up of public investment in renewables and energy efficiency, seek to mobilise EU society to adopt sufficiency-focused ways of life, and announce the redeployment of a segment of the EU workforce to renovate tens of millions of buildings every year. Their motives are different: the left underlines the need to invest so as to help the Europeans who face the greatest difficulties, while liberals see in this transformation the best economic model for an ever-greener and digitalised global economy, and national "patriots" see this as a national security priority in order to deprive Vladimir Putin and other aggressive fossil fuel autocrats of their biggest asset in modern-day geopolitics.

With such large-scale consensus, the next president of the Commission secures unanimous support in the European Council for a new EU joint borrowing programme that funds an EU long-term climate investment plan. The objective is no longer to ensure minor growth in cleantech sectors, but to make Europe the 21st-century "Green Arsenal of Democracy". Just as it only took a few years for Franklin Roosevelt's United States to massively scale up armaments production during World War II, the EU manages a tenfold increase in the production of wind power systems, insulation materials and heat pumps in only four years. It also doubles its research and development investments, leading to a few breakthrough technologies in areas such as osmotic energy, material alternatives to critical metals and carbon-negative materials, clearing the way for another decade of energy and industrial transformation.

Despite this massive green industrialisation, the EU energy demand shrinks. The most socially dubious and energy-intensive consumption patterns disappear and energy sufficiency becomes the new social norm. This change is driven by influencers who underline the positive health effects of eating less meat, walking and biking, taking cold showers – and also by religious and philosophical movements who emphasise the spiritual values of modesty and humility, as well as sufficiency practices. As meat consumption shrinks, a lot of EU land is now available to increase the production of crops for renewable energy purposes, and the production of food for a Global South that further suffers from climate change. Agricultural water consumption is also reduced, which allows for a modest increase in the water consumption of the new cleantech factories, such as hydrogen production facilities.

To fund this transition and fight inflation, an exceptional tax on corporate profits, a billionaires' contribution and a financial transactions tax are introduced. The political families that traditionally opposed those measures accept them as temporary ones, with an integrated sunset clause of 5–10 years. Each within their remit, the European Central Bank, the European Investment Bank and national promotional banks furthermore ensure a very low cost of capital and generously fund green projects

– while the EU capital markets union is on the verge of being achieved, which would ensure that cheap private capital can take over.

To overcome skill shortages, trade unions accept temporary measures that increase the EU legal maximum working time to more than 50 hours per week. Several member states introduce "green draft legislations", whereby 10% of each generation volunteers or is drafted to perform two years of civil service focused on green and secure-energy projects. After that service, most of them continue a career in a green transition sector. Green workers benefit from an elevated social status, with installers of heat pumps or photovoltaic roofs being as celebrated as nurses were during the worst moment of the 2020 Covid pandemic, further attracting workers of all ages into those fields. The EU introduces a special "Green Visa" that benefits 1 million migrant workers, giving them the security of a five-year work permit in green economy sectors, and the choice after five years to stay in Europe or go, with a financial bonus, to a third country in the hope that they can start their own green economy business there, further strengthening the cultural and economic ties between the EU and the Global South.

Sustaining Europe's green leadership

Those two extremely divergent scenarios are both unlikely to materialise. Yet they outline some of the main challenges that will shape the agenda during the next mandate of the European Parliament and Commission, and the consequent priorities for EU bodies and member states.

The transformation of the EU energy system requires massive amounts of investments that only yield an economic return in the long term, from offshore wind parks to building renovation. The economic profitability and feasibility of those projects will therefore very much depend on the cost of capital. The higher the cost of capital, the fewer and less profitable green investments will be. Policymakers should therefore monitor the cost of capital for these projects and adopt policies that can help decrease it. Such policies include more assertive public banks (to keep interest rates low for green projects), the finalisation of the EU capital markets union and public financial instruments.

Making energy sufficiency mainstream and avoiding it becoming a culture war topic will be critical. Every winter, each member state should launch a public information campaign aimed at saving energy, especially around heating. The efficiency of each campaign should be monitored each year, drawing lessons for the next. Sufficiency can indeed play a major role in curbing the emergence of new pollution-intensive ways of life – such as the emergence in the last 15 years of SUVs and low-cost aviation as the new norm. It can also deliver speedy reductions in fossil fuel consumption, as well as reducing the investment needs for the transition; for example, a smaller and cheaper heat pump might suffice to heat the same home at 18 °C rather than 22 °C.

The Green Deal coalition should be broadened by adding to its existing economic and climate narrative a narrative that addresses more forcefully issues of energy security, defence and geopolitics. Such a narrative would be politically efficient, as it would speak to constituencies who tend not to list climate among their top political priorities. It could also lead to the adoption of new policies geared towards ensuring secure access to critical materials for the EU, and international cooperation to reduce oil and gas consumption, as a means to further damage Putin's capacity to turn his oil and gas into cash and weapons to wage his war on Ukraine.

EU and national leaders should plan the phase-out of fossil fuel subsidies and build a political consensus around the need for a long-term EU climate investment plan. Such long-term investment can provide tangible support to member states, local authorities, small and medium-sized enterprises and families who may struggle to identify and fund the clean energy investment projects they need. While not being a silver bullet, such a long-term EU climate investment plan could be the key climate recommendation to present to EU citizens in the context of the EU elections, and both a funding and a governance tool to articulate EU, national and private sector investments in a way that furthers cooperation between the EU and member states and between the public and private sectors. It can also become a tool to derisk projects and lower the cost of capital, as well as a way of funding the infrastructures that would give Europeans the freedom to opt for a sufficient lifestyle (such as bike lanes and railways). With the approaching EU elections of May 2024 and the end of Next-GenerationEU in sight, such a long-term climate investment plan could ensure that EU, national and private investments turn all the Green Deal objectives into tangible realities for businesses, workers and families.

George Papaconstantinou

4 | The global economic disorder: drifting towards fragmentation

The full-scale Russian invasion of Ukraine has undoubtedly redrawn the global geopolitical and geoeconomic map. Irrespective of the outcome of the military operations, the invasion has raised the spectre of a new and long-lasting Iron Curtain, separating the West, broadly defined, from Russia and China, and generating serious political and economic risks for a large part of the Global South. The far-reaching implications of several rounds of economic sanctions adopted by the US, Europe and their partners seem to have taken preexisting cleavages and fragmentation in the world economy to a new level.

A new global economic environment is taking shape. There are too many uncertainties to fully flesh out its characteristics, but it is still worth exploring the possible emerging shape of global economic governance. Two sets of questions are central to this exercise. First, what kind of leverage does the West have, and how much will it be able to maintain, over the "plumbing" of global economic interdependence, including finance, trade and investment? And second, what does the further widening of economic fragmentation entail for the ability of the international community to provide global public goods (such as climate security and health) or for the preservation of the global digital infrastructure?

Answers to these questions are by no means straightforward, nor can they be deterministic. Sketching them out requires several steps. The first is to assess whether in fact the war represents a "break", a major discontinuity in global economic governance. The first section of this chapter briefly reviews how the architecture of the multilateral system has evolved over time. The second section discusses the drivers of this shift: the shaping factors and, more specifically, the impact of the widespread economic sanctions adopted by the West in response to the Russian invasion of Ukraine. The third section then outlines different scenarios ahead, ranging from a relatively benign one of managed multipolarity to a scenario of collapsing multilateralism. Finally, the fourth section focuses on the role of the EU in this brave new world and attempts to draw some policy conclusions and prescriptions.

In search of a global economic order: cascading blows to a precarious edifice

The full-scale invasion of Ukraine and the current war are bound to accelerate the fragmentation of the international economic order and increase uncertainty about the future of the global economic governance framework. In particular, the ability of the latter to ensure that economic interdependence delivers stability, shared prosperity and global public goods is being tested as never before. The geopolitical chasm opened by the war has injected further mistrust among the main global players and turned many policy areas into arenas of open contestation. However, the war in Ukraine has not disrupted an otherwise stable and effective global economic order. It rather exacerbates trends and drivers of change that had already been at play, and that pointed to an expanding governance deficit in the face of growing (geo)political tensions.

It is doubtful whether there was ever really a golden age of global governance. The framework of governance rules and institutions was never comprehensive enough to adequately cover the multiple and increasingly complex channels of economic interdependence, and the "rules-based" regime was never entirely rules-based. Institutional arrangements have long been playing catch-up with reality. Global economic governance has continuously morphed, attempting to adapt – successfully or less so – to evolving structures of economic interdependence or to geopolitical shifts and power struggles. And the attempt after the fall of the Berlin Wall to invent a new international rulebook on the back of an "end of history" assumption, anticipating convergence around market-based capitalism and democratic values, did not survive long.

The narrative of the "end of globalisation" has increasingly accompanied the debate about the inadequacies of global economic governance. Globalisation has been challenged by a combination of social discontent, political opposition and geopolitical rivalry. But the data show a mixed picture. World trade as a percentage of gross domestic product (GDP) has stalled since about 2005, and although external liabilities (debt, foreign direct investment, other financial obligations owed to nonresidents) have increased much faster than trade, they too have recently stabilised as a percentage of GDP. Talk about deglobalisation is therefore premature, but cracks in the fabric of global economic interdependence have been widening for many years, well before the spread of the Covid pandemic and the outbreak of the war in Ukraine.

Signs of fragmentation included the generalised reassertion of sovereignty, the abuse of US hyperpower, populism, the weakening of democracies, the rise of authoritarianism, and differences between advanced and developing countries concerning issue of fairness in the global economy and the terms of global economic governance. Besides, many commentators had already focused on the "return of geopolitics", challenging the primacy of the prevailing and dominant economic perspective for managing globalisation.[1]

Recent work on fragmentation of investment flows shows vividly how flows of foreign direct investment are increasingly concentrated among geopolitically aligned countries, particularly in strategic sectors.[2] It also illustrates the dangers entailed by a policy-driven reversal of global economic integration, with technological decoupling amplifying losses from trade restrictions, and with emerging market economies and low-income countries likely to be most at risk. Recent projections estimate that costs to global output from trade fragmentation might rise to 7% of GDP in a severe fragmentation scenario, and to 8–10% if technological decoupling is factored in.[3]

---

1 Pisani-Ferry, J. (2023), argues that geopolitics and international economics have long operated under two distinct paradigms: a zero-sum game for foreign policy experts and the potential from multilateral cooperation and market-led integration for mutual gains seen by economists ("The economic threat of undisciplined geopolitical primacy", *Project Syndicate*, 1 May; https://www.project-syndicate.org/commentary/prioritizing-geopolitics-over-economic-prosperity-severe-consequences-by-jean-pisani-ferry-2023-05). These increasingly contrasting views are encapsulated in a characteristic sentence from Harris, J., and Sullivan, J. (2020): "Today's national security experts need to move beyond the prevailing neoliberal economic philosophy of the past 40 years" ("America needs a new economic philosophy: foreign policy experts can help", *Foreign Policy*, 7 February; https://foreignpolicy.com/2020/02/07/america-needs-a-new-economic-philosophy-foreign-policy-experts-can-help/).

2 IMF (2023) "Geoeconomic fragmentation and foreign direct investment". Chapter 4 in "World economic outlook: a rocky recovery", IMF, April (https://www.imf.org/en/Publications/WEO/Issues/2023/04/11/world-economic-outlook-april-2023).

3 Aiyar, S., Chen, J., Ebeke, C. H., et al. (2023) "Geoeconomic fragmentation and the future of multilateralism". IMF Staff Discussion Note 2023/1 (https://www.imf.org/en/Publications/Staff-Discussion-Notes/Issues/2023/01/11/Geo-Economic-Fragmentation-and-the-Future-of-Multilateralism-527266). This IMF research report examines and attempts to quantify the adverse consequences of geoeconomic fragmentation across a number of fields.

And yet the imperative of global collective action has never been so strong across a number of policy fields. These include the basic flows of international interdependence – trade in goods and services, financial flows – as well as "behind the border" integration (namely, competition policy on a global scale, regulation of banking and finance, and international taxation) and the critical area of global public goods (health and climate, as well as the global digital infrastructure).[4]

Perhaps the biggest problems are in international trade and investment, which represent the basic "plumbing" of international economic interdependence and the backbone of global prosperity. Multilateral trade principles are being challenged by a combination of US unilateralism, Chinese assertiveness and the prevalence of preferential trade agreements. The regime for international investment flows is fragmenting, and the global financial safety net provided by the International Monetary Fund (IMF) is giving way to overlapping financial safety nets that include bilateral lending, regional safety nets and self-insurance, raising questions about global financial stability.[5]

Economic interdependence also increasingly involves regulation "behind the border". This concerns the juxtaposition between the operation of global firms across borders and their regulation through national competition regimes that are loosely coordinated and struggle with extraterritoriality. It also relates to the problems of financial regulation of global banks, in a system relying on a loose coordinate-and-review mechanism and on a global financial regulatory regime facing new challenges from shadow banking and digital finance. To this should be added the challenge of the governance of international taxation, for which new rules

---

[4] An analysis of the "state of governance" in different policy fields can be found in Papaconstantinou, G., and Pisani-Ferry, J. (2021) "New rules for a new world: a survival kit", STG Policy Analysis 2021/09 (https://cadmus.eui.eu/handle/1814/71069); and in Papaconstantinou, G., and Pisani-Ferry, J. (eds) (2022) "New world, new rules? Final report on the transformation of global governance project 2018–2021", European University Institute (https://cadmus.eui.eu/handle/1814/74829). The latter was the outcome of a three-year project undertaken at the European University Institute on the transformation of global governance.

[5] See, for example, the recent speech by European Central Bank President Christine Lagarde, "Central banks in a fragmenting world", at the Council on Foreign Relations' C. Peter McColough Series on International Economics, 17 April 2023 (https://www.ecb.europa.eu/press/key/date/2023/html/ecb.sp230417~9f8d34fbd6.en.html); or earlier analytical work by Claessens, S. (2019) "Fragmentation in global financial markets: good or bad for financial stability?", BIS Working Paper 815, 1 October (https://www.bis.org/publ/work815.htm). In that paper, Claessens examines the implications of fragmentation in global financial markets for financial stability.

have had to be invented for tax cooperation in a policy area that is at the core of national sovereignty.

The governance deficit is particularly evident in the delivery of global public goods, such as public health and the environment. Compared with economic flows, these are relatively recent areas of international cooperation, and the global community has struggled to devise effective governance frameworks. The difficulties were plain to see with the absence of global disease prevention when Covid hit. They are also evident when dealing with the hardest of all collective action problems, climate change, for which a combination of voluntary national commitments and action by the private sector is supposed to carry the momentum of mitigation and adaptation. And we are only now realising the issues inherent in preserving a global digital infrastructure in the face of its weaponisation, of concerns over privacy, and of tech giants abusing their dominant positions.

The Covid pandemic and Russia's full-scale invasion of Ukraine have dealt a double blow to the already precarious edifice of global economic governance. The pandemic disrupted global supply chains, trade and investment, brought global public health to the forefront of the policy debate, and helped reinforce the understanding of the impact of human behaviour on our natural environment. The current war in Ukraine is a major geopolitical event with direct implications for energy and food supplies, as well as for trade and investment. The drastic sanction packages adopted by the West against Russia add a new dimension to global fragmentation and carry important global knock-on effects for the global economic (dis)order beyond their impact on the aggressor.

The impact of the war in Ukraine and economic sanctions on the global economic order

Alongside military assistance, economic sanctions against Russia form a two-pronged strategy put in place by the West to defeat Russia's military aggression. The aim of the sanctions is to impose economic and political costs on the Russian political elite responsible for the invasion, weaken Russia's economic base, and effectively cripple the Russian regime's ability to wage war.[6] To do so, the West is leveraging its control of the infrastructure of globalisation. It does so through the global financial

---

6 Details on the ten EU packages adopted can be found at https://finance.ec.europa .eu/eu-and-world/sanctions-restrictive-measures/sanctions-adopted-following-russias -military-aggression-against-ukraine_en.

plumbing, by excluding Russia from the use of clearing houses and the SWIFT financial transaction system, by excluding it from the use of currencies such as the dollar and the euro for transactions and settlements, by limiting its access to the global digital infrastructure, and by excluding it from global value chains in key sectors.

Following the imposition of 11 rounds of sanctions, the list in the case of the EU is of unprecedented scope. In addition to travel bans on individuals and asset freezes on individuals and entities, economic sanctions mainly target the financial sector: a SWIFT ban for Russian banks; a freeze on foreign assets, and a prohibition on transactions with the Russian central bank; a restriction on access to EU primary and secondary capital markets for Russian banks and companies; a prohibition on providing euro-denominated banknotes to Russia; a prohibition on public financing or investment in Russia; and a ban on providing crypto wallets.[7]

It is too early to draw a proper assessment of the sanctions' effectiveness in forcing Russia to change course and stop the war, but historical evidence invites caution. A seminal study based on more than 200 recorded instances suggests that the correlation between economic deprivation caused by sanctions and the political willingness of sanctioned countries to change course is weak.[8] Sanctions are more likely to succeed when the goal is relatively modest and the target country is economically weak and politically unstable, and economic sanctions often need to be accompanied by military action to be successful. Recent analysis suggests that, following the initial disruptive shock on the Russian financial system from the widespread sanctions, the economy has stabilised and adapted. Medium- and long-term prospects are, however, decidedly worse as a result of sanctions, not least because of the departure of a

---

7   Beyond the financial sector, sanctions cover energy (prohibitions on oil and coal imports from Russia, on exports to Russia of goods and technologies used in oil refining, and on new investments in the Russian energy sector), transport (the closure of EU airspace, ports and roads to all Russian aircraft, vessels and transport operators, and bans on exports to Russia of goods and technology used in the aviation, maritime and space sectors), defence (a ban on exports to Russia of dual-use goods and tech, and on trade in arms), raw materials and other goods (bans on luxury goods exports to Russia and imports of iron, steel, wood, cement, etc.), and services (a ban on providing IT, consulting, legal, engineering and similar services).

8   Hufbauer, G. C., Schott, J. J., Elliott, K. A., et al. (2009) *Economic Sanctions Reconsidered*, 3rd edition (Washington, DC: Peterson Institute for International Economics).

large number of foreign firms, with the Russian economy settling at a lower equilibrium.[9]

The broader question is the impact of sanctions on the global economic order over time. Sanctions are, after all, blunt instruments that often produce unintended and undesirable consequences, which can go beyond their immediate target. Understanding these requires looking at the state of play across several policy areas, and notably in the financial sector, energy and technology. This would allow us to have a sense of how the West's leverage over the international economic order may evolve, and of the potential side-effects of sanctions in an environment where attitudes towards Russia's invasion of Ukraine around the world are at best mixed.

The financial sector has been the main target of sanctions. The West has harnessed its dominance in world currency markets – with the dollar and the euro together accounting for almost 80% of the stock of global foreign exchange reserves, over 80% of outstanding international debt securities, close to 70% of outstanding international loans, over 60% of international deposits and 80% of daily foreign exchange trading. But sanctions are a strong incentive to diversify reserves.

The only possible alternative to the dominance of the dollar and the euro is the Chinese renminbi. Sanctions are indeed likely to accelerate the internationalisation of RMB, although data do not yet show significant movements in this direction. It is, however, in this context, and in light of successive G7 commitments to curtail Russia's use of the international financial system,[10] that one should understand Russia adopting the renminbi as one of the main currencies for its international reserves and trade,[11] as well as interpret statements about alternatives to the dollar from other countries, including the BRICS (Brazil, Russia, India, China and

---

9 For a comprehensive analysis of the macroeconomic implications of Western sanctions on Russia, see Demertzis, M., Hilgenstock, B., McWilliams, B., et al. (2022) "How have sanctions impacted Russia?" Bruegel Policy Contribution 18/22, October (https://www.bruegel.org/policy-brief/how-have-sanctions-impacted-russia).

10 From the recent "G7 leaders' statement on Ukraine", 19 May 2023 (https://www.consilium.europa.eu/en/press/press-releases/2023/05/19/g7-leaders-statement-on-ukraine/).

11 See Stognei, A. (2023) "Russia embraces China's renminbi in face of western sanctions". *Financial Times*, 26 March (https://www.ft.com/content/65681143-c6af-4b64-827d-a7ca6171937a).

South Africa) exploring "the potential use of alternative currencies to the current internationally traded currencies".[12]

In addition to weaponising currency,[13] the West has implemented a SWIFT ban for most Russian banks, thereby depriving them of the platform for messaging international interbank transactions. But while at the outset this was considered a radical move, it has proved less consequential than expected. Reasons vary: SWIFT is a messaging platform, not a clearing platform, and only selected Russian banks have been cut off from SWIFT, not all of them. In addition, the impact on domestic confidence in terms of withdrawals and bank runs was partly neutralised by the Russian central bank, which, since 2014, had been developing its own system for transmitting financial messages to mitigate the fallout of the potential exclusion of Russia from SWIFT. Russia has also been conducting nondollar financial transactions using alternative messaging services with China and has expanded nondollar financial transactions with the Gulf and India.

Asset freezes have been another important tool. Aside from targeting the assets of individuals, what has been groundbreaking was freezing about 40% of the reserves of the Central Bank of Russia held as deposits with other central banks, the Bank for International Settlements or the IMF. These reserves are important both because almost 80% of Russian trade has traditionally been settled in euros or dollars and because they are used for paying external debt. However, the impact of the asset freezes has been partly mitigated by the fact that – despite their declining revenue path – energy exports continue to bring in necessary foreign currency.

One important question relates to whether financial sanctions against Russia will act as the turning point for a redrawing of the global financial system. While there is evidence of diversification, a full realignment away from the dollar (and euro) denominated system is not in sight. China's unquestionable rising importance in international trade and finance is not the only factor determining whether a new China-centred system

---

12 As quoted by South Africa's foreign minister Naledi Pandor in Roelf, W. (2023) "BRICS ministers put on show of strength as Putin arrest warrant looms large", *Reuters*, 1 June. See also Leahy, J., and Lockett, H. (2023) "Brazil's Lula calls for end to dollar trade dominance", *Financial Times*, 13 April (https://www.ft.com/content/669260a5-82a5-4e7a-9bbf-4f41c54a6143).

13 For an analytical approach on the concept and practice of "weaponised interdependence", see Farrell, H., and Newman, A. (2019) "Weaponized interdependence: how global economic networks shape state coercion". *International Security*, 44(1): 42–79. DOI: 10.1162/ISEC_a_00351

emerges. Whether other countries adopt the renminbi as a main currency for international reserves or switch to a Chinese financial messaging system largely depends on perceptions about Chinese policies in these domains. Fears of unpredictable currency shifts and a lack of legal certainty in transactions continue to linger and may prove an insurmountable obstacle for such a shift.

It is in this context that one should also see the ongoing discussions concerning Russian asset freezes. Decisions to use profits from currently frozen assets or even to outright appropriate these assets to pay for the costs of the war and the reconstruction of Ukraine have a solid moral footing. At the same time, they are fraught with legal difficulties; what is more, they may undermine the confidence in the Western-dominated rules-based system of international financial transactions and accelerate a move away from it.[14]

Energy sanctions have been the most contested of these measures among EU member states, given European reliance on Russian gas, but they may also prove the most effective, given the importance of energy export revenues for the Russian economy. For gas in particular, in the short term the European capacity to diversify has been remarkable. In the longer term the sanctions will likely accelerate Europe's exit from gas, and Russia will become dependent on Chinese and other markets, adding to the fragmentation of the global energy market.

Technology sanctions are also worth mentioning. Even though the US and EU export very little to Russia, the export controls instituted have been emulated by other countries in the Western alliance, though not necessarily more broadly. A ban on technology exports to Russia, however, has global effects on the behaviour of multinational companies and exporters and in some cases has direct effects on third countries such as China, to the extent that these bans impact Western behaviour

---

14 An "options paper" by the European Commission on the use of frozen assets to support Ukraine's reconstruction can be found at https://www.politico.eu/wp-content/uploads/2023/02/07/Use-of-assets-option-paper_19-Nov-2022_final_clean.docx. For a discussion of these issues, see Demertzis, M. (2023) "Bank of Russia's immobilised assets: what happens next?", Bruegel wesbite, May (https://www.bruegel.org/comment/bank-russias-immobilised-assets-what-happens-next).

towards the global operation of Chinese or other third-country firms that export to Russia.[15]

In addition to aiming to isolate the Russian economy from the world economic system and reduce Russia's ability to wage war, sanctions also result in further fragmentation of that system. Whether in trade, finance or technology, sanctions reinforce preexisting cleavages and create new ones. They encourage third countries such as China – but also India and other mid-sized powers in Asia, Africa and Latin America – to look for alternative global economic governance solutions.[16] In addition, to the extent that fragmentation "spills over", they may therefore make it harder for the international community to cooperate in preserving global public goods such as climate, health and digital infrastructure.

For the time being, and despite the political rhetoric, regional financial safety arrangements do not add up to an alternative global governance framework. Nor have the tensions shaping geoeconomic competition so far disrupted climate negotiations (though additional mistrust in global health governance as well as in managing the global digital infrastructure is plainly evident). For an alternative global governance system centred around China to emerge, it would require significant strengthening of China's geopolitical position coupled with a refusal by the West to accommodate China's desire – and the desire of a wide range of emerging countries – for a bigger stake in current governance arrangements.

Looking ahead: between fragmentation and fracture

On the basis of the existing geoeconomic situation and the likely impact of economic sanctions on Russia, it is possible to sketch a number of alternative scenarios ahead. This is a perilous exercise at the best of times. Given the uncertainties regarding the actual outcome of the war,

---

15   Chorzempa, M. (2022) "New technology restrictions against Russia could also target China". *Realtime Economics* blog, Peterson Institute for International Economics, 7 March (https://www.piie.com/blogs/realtime-economic-issues-watch/new-technology-restrictions-against-russia-could-also-target). Chorzempa examines the impact of US technology restrictions against Russia on China and concludes that the international community has effectively made export controls more legitimate as a tool to punish outliers.

16   An important part of creating alternative global economic governance solutions involves China's attempts to dethrone the dollar. A recent example of this discussion is found in Liu, Z. Z. (2022) "China is quietly trying to dethrone the dollar". *Foreign Policy*, 21 September (https://foreignpolicy.com/2022/09/21/china-yuan-us-dollar-sco-currency/).

it becomes even more so. Nevertheless, one can think of four possible scenarios, from the more benign to the downright catastrophic.

Scenario 1: a reinforced status quo ante

For a while during Covid, voices arguing for a "new Bretton Woods" could be heard, as the world realised that preventing or managing pandemics was the kind of problem that required global coordination and that the tools and institutions in place were not up to the task. But that moment came and went. Instead, nationalisms and narrow political expediency took over, and Russia's attack on Ukraine exacerbated them.

A reinforced "status quo ante" would entail political decisions to finish the job of creating a multilateral economic governance framework. In terms of organisations, it would involve, among other things, funding the IMF to be able to act as a lender of last resort in new crises, resolving the problems around the functioning of the World Trade Organization, giving the World Health Organization political clout and enforcement capabilities, creating a global competition authority, returning to the abandoned Multilateral Agreement on Investment, giving more power to the Financial Stability Board, funding a global environment agency, and making the G20 more representative and effective. None of these developments are about to happen; this scenario can only serve as a reference of sorts.

Scenario 2: multipolarity prevails

Multipolarity has been the state of affairs for some time now, with three large economic blocs – the US, China and the EU – competing across all policy dimensions: trade, investment and technology. This framework combines imperfectly functioning organisations that are anchored in hard law and multilateral principles with emergent governance regimes characterised by soft law and cooperation among variable coalitions in different policy areas.

This scenario suggests more of the same: a continuation of global economic governance as it has evolved over the last decades. In fields such as climate, taxation, global competition, and even digital and international banking supervision, it might indeed be possible to shelter governance frameworks from systemic competition and geopolitical rivalry. It is, however, difficult to imagine this happening in the traditional fields of interdependence: namely, trade and capital flows. Trade rules do not command anymore the universal support they once enjoyed.[17] Similarly, the near-universal consensus on the principles of international credit has been shattered by the rise of China's overseas lending, and transparency is blatantly lacking.[18] Problems in these fields will only be exacerbated following the war in Ukraine.

Scenario 3: fragmentation squared

The previous scenario suggests that the multipolarity that has emerged over the last decades can settle into a "new normal" buttressed by a (loose) set of rules and withstand geopolitical rivalries. But this is probably too optimistic. Trade and finance are two areas where governance rules have broken down with no viable alternatives in sight.

As fragmentation in these domains progresses, it is difficult to think that governance problems will not "spill over" to other, currently less contested policy areas. Digital is an obvious one, where the multistakeholder model is already under strain from systemic rivalry over technological leadership as well as from different preferences in areas such as data privacy.[19] International tax governance is another. The advances made in this area through the Organisation for Economic Co-operation and Development (OECD) relied on a clear political push by the G20, which this format may not be able to deliver in future. Banking supervision and competition policy are also policy areas where the governance framework in place may not prove sustainable if systemic rivalry pollutes the soft coordinate-and-review method that applies in the banking sector and the set of principles shared by national competition authorities breaks down. But perhaps the biggest dangers lie in the area of climate governance, simply because the stakes there are so high.

---

17 On this, see Rodrik, D. (2018) "What do trade agreements really do?" *Journal of Economic Perspectives*, 32(2): 73–90.

18 See Gelpern, A., Horn, S., Morris, S., et al. (2021) "How China lends: a rare look into 100 debt contracts with foreign governments". Report, Peterson Institute for International Economics, Kiel Institute for the World Economy, Center for Global Development and AidData at William & Mary (https://www.aiddata.org/publications/how-china-lends).

19 This has prompted the members of the G7 to signal that they "affirm the importance to address common governance challenges and to identify potential gaps and fragmentation in global technology governance". See "G7 Hiroshima leaders' communiqué", 20 May 2023 (https://www.consilium.europa.eu/en/press/press-releases/2023/05/20/g7-hiroshima-leaders-communique/).

Scenario 4: fracture – a new Iron Curtain

The most likely turn of events is probably positioned between the second, "benign multipolarity" scenario and the more problematic third one, envisaging further fragmentation. But this assumes that the geopolitical rivalry does not escalate well beyond its current confines. It is not difficult to see how this could come about, through disruptive events such as the direct involvement of the West in the war in Ukraine – for example, following the use of weapons of mass destruction by Russia – or China attacking Taiwan.

In any such event, the fragmentation scenario would quickly degenerate into a full-blown fracture – a new Iron Curtain pitting the West against the rest. Globalisation would be fully disrupted, and with it any semblance of global economic governance rules. Global supply chains would need to be completely rethought in an environment of trade rules fully subject to national security considerations, foreign investment flows drastically curtailed and redirected, and a fully partitioned internet. Geopolitical competition would undermine efforts to deliver global public goods, future pandemics would spread through the cracks of a crumbling international health governance system and climate targets would become much harder to achieve. A truly dystopian future.

The role of the EU: derisking in a world of fragmentation

The EU has always been a rules-based entity, and a strong proponent of the multilateral system. It is, however, facing a situation where China and the US do not separate economic interests from geopolitical ones as the EU has done.[20] From trade to investment and digital, the US has taken a national-security-based approach, identifying China as a systemic rival. Traditionally the guarantor of the multilateral system, it is now challenging some of its main precepts, in a shift outlasting the Trump administration. China, on the other hand, has made it clear that it intends to assert its own central role in the global governance system and rewrite its rules in ways that match its interests. Beijing is using a combination of means to that end, from trade relations to its trademark Belt and Road initiative and large-scale bilateral lending. It has also backed Russia's narrative on the

---

20 The argument is developed in Pisani-Ferry, J., Wolff, G., Shapiro, J., et al. (2019) "Redefining Europe's sovereignty". Bruegel Policy Contribution 9, June (https://www.bruegel.org/policy-brief/redefining-europes-economic-sovereignty).

responsibilities of the West in triggering the war and de facto provided vital political, diplomatic and economic backing to Russia.

This leaves the EU as the only global power that is playing by multilateral rules in a world that has become more complicated and conflictual after the war in Ukraine. The EU has sided with the US in putting together the extensive economic sanctions in place against Russia. But it is not necessarily ready to follow the US in a strategy of "decoupling" from China, especially when it sees the US reshoring and friendshoring important areas of economic activity and, with its recent Inflation Reduction Act, pursuing a "Made in America" strategy in the race for new clean technologies. In a world where not all mineral resources are equally distributed and not all productive technologies are equally available, there is a strong economic case for investing in respective comparative advantages and pursuing some specialisation along global value chains. However, the question for the EU is whether – in a highly contested world, where economics and politics are increasingly interwoven – rivalry and economic integration can coexist and, if so, under which terms.

The EU has for some time now been pivoting from a focus on internal integration towards external action, attempting to develop policies to "shape globalisation".[21] It attempted to navigate Covid and the war in Ukraine through developing the idea of "open strategic autonomy", roughly understood as "the capacity to cope alone if necessary but without ruling out cooperation whenever possible", and ranging from developing the international role of the euro, to extraterritorial support for EU companies operating globally, to technology and global supply chain management.[22] More recently, the EU has sought to articulate a narrative around the alternative notion of "derisking", seeking to enhance

---

[21] The declaration on globalisation published in the annex of the European Council statement of December 2007 includes the sentences: "Globalisation is increasingly shaping our lives [...] We aim at shaping globalisation in the interests of all our citizens, based on our common values and principles." See also the lecture by Pisani-Ferry at the EUI State of the Union, reproduced in Papaconstantinou, G., and Pisani-Ferry, J. (eds) (2022) "New world, new rules?", in which some of the arguments in this section are further developed.

[22] See, for example, Cagnin, C., Muench, S., Scapolo, F., et al. (2021) "Shaping and securing the EU's Open Strategic Autonomy by 2040 and beyond". EUR 30802 EN, Joint Research Centre, European Commission (https://publications.jrc.ec.europa.eu/repository/handle/JRC125994).

resilience while preserving the basic tools and frameworks of the system of global governance.[23]

The aim is to advance derisking through policies that address supply chains (including those crucial to energy security), critical infrastructures and technology. To achieve these goals the EU would utilise trade and investment instruments such as the newly adopted Anti-coercion Instrument and International Procurement Instrument, and the existing Foreign Direct Investment Screening Regulation. Consideration is also being given to defining a list of strategically important technologies to curtail critical technology transfers, and to a stronger export-control regime for dual-use goods.[24]

In this direction, there are some general policy principles that should guide the EU's derisking approach. The starting point is to understand that, while the clear delineation between economic policy and geopolitics is no longer operative, it is still important to define how and when security-related considerations can and should be taken on board in policy areas where decisions should continue to be based primarily on economic principles (such as competition policy, currencies and investment decisions). This suggests a circumspect and careful use of the policy instruments mentioned above.

Another policy principle is to confront some inescapable trade-offs between preserving global public goods and economic integration. An example: the introduction of a Carbon Border Adjustment Mechanism addresses in practice an existing trade-off between climate preservation and trade promotion while preserving basic trade principles.

A third principle is the need to better connect EU integration with external action. To take an example, it is well understood that projecting the global power of the euro is an important component of strengthening the EU's global competitiveness and preserving its economic power.[25] But doing so is simply not possible without a completed economic and monetary union, an integrated capital market and a common EU safe

---

23 See the recent speech by the president of the European Commission: von der Leyen, U. (2023) "Speech by President von der Leyen on EU–China relations to the Mercator Institute for China Studies and the European Policy Centre". European Commission website, 30 March (https://ec.europa.eu/commission/presscorner/detail/en/speech_23_2063).

24 See European Commission (2023) "An EU approach to enhance economic security". Joint Communication, 20 June (https://eur-lex.europa.eu/legal-content/EN/TXT/PDF/?uri=CELEX:52023JC0020).

25 For an analysis, see Papaconstantinou, G. (2023) "Strengthening the global role of the euro". FEPS Polic-y Brief, April (https://feps-europe.eu/wp-content/uploads/2023/04/Strengthening-the-global-role-of-the-Euro.pdf).

asset. These are part of equipping the EU with the right policy framework and instruments to play an economic role that befits its high geopolitical ambitions in the new world.

Finally, it is important to recognise that narrowly defined European interests will sometimes clash with the goal of maintaining a functioning multilateral system, and great care will need to go into balancing competing objectives. The EU will need to take a broad view of its long-term interest in the preservation of a rules-based international economic order. This includes recognising that, for multipolarity to not degenerate into extreme fragmentation, global institutions need to regain legitimacy in the eyes of much of the non-Western world. This will require a rebalancing in the representation of different regions and blocs in multilateral bodies, sometimes as a quid pro quo for retaining their role in upholding and reforming shared norms and principles.

Elvire Fabry

5 | Global trade and investment: the rising economic security paradigm

The Covid-19 pandemic abruptly interrupted supply chains and slowed international investment flows, making supply chain resilience a priority. But, with the war in Ukraine and intensifying rivalry between the US and China, the accumulation of major external shocks calls for more than just recovering from unexpected disruptions. The challenge is systemic, and it requires adapting to a new, more complex and unstable international system. The use of economic coercion for geopolitical ends is leading to a profound disruption of globalisation. It is far from clear how economic interdependence will be managed, or how fragmented globalisation will become.

By early 2022 the return to pre-Covid trends contradicted the deglobalisation scenario that some had anticipated. Instead, it is the full-scale invasion of Ukraine that will likely be remembered as having provoked a decisive reorganisation of globalisation – one aimed at reducing risks associated with geopolitical rivalries. The most consequential driver of change is less the immediate impact of the war than the acceleration of the Sino-American rivalry that it provoked, which is leading to greater efforts to reduce excessive dependence on any individual supplier. Besides, as the war continues, further market disruptions in the short to medium term cannot be ruled out. If Chinese President Xi Jinping were to add military equipment to China's current economic support for Vladimir Putin, that would underscore the need to disengage further from Chinese supply chains.

It has probably never been so challenging to build scenarios on the evolution of global trade while economic nationalism is taking hold. The multiplication of economic security strategies around the world illustrates the growing uncertainty. At this stage it is probably not very realistic to envisage a cooperative scenario of greater openness of the Chinese market, reengagement of the United States in the World Trade Organization and the strengthening of the regulation of globalisation through new agreements. Current developments point to different degrees of fragmentation in the global trade order, which poses major challenges for Europeans. Despite their continued commitment to a rules-based system and to new multilateral negotiations, Europeans are not in the driver's seat of the ongoing transformation of globalisation. It is the initiatives of the United States and China that are setting the agenda for this reshuffling. But Europeans are on the front line, very much exposed to the war at their borders and to the risks linked to their strong dependence on Chinese demand and supply.

The war in Ukraine and the acceleration of reglobalisation

The new record high in the value of global trade flows reached in 2022, at $32 trillion, corresponds to an economic rebound following the disruption caused by the pandemic. There has been no major reduction in the geographic distances covered by value chains. Measures to strengthen their resilience have sometimes meant seeking out suppliers further afield. As some countries recovered quicker than others from the pandemic disruptions, accessing markets where demand is stronger has also meant looking for more remote markets.

The immediate impact of the invasion of Ukraine on global trade and investment has been curbed by the relatively minor role that Russia and Ukraine play in the global economy, except for certain agricultural and industrial goods. The war has, however, affected logistics networks at the regional and global scales.[1] Besides disruptions in the Black Sea region, the reciprocal closure of airspace between Russia and 36 countries is stretching trade routes and raising prices for air freight between Europe and East Asia. Around 20% of global air cargo has been affected by airspace bans.[2] Commodity markets (especially food and energy) have seen a sharp surge in prices, but overall trade volumes have remained rather stable, with meaningful trade diversion taking place to

---

[1] Ruta, M. (2022) "The impact of the war in Ukraine on global trade and investment". Report, World Bank, April.
[2] Guénette, J.-D., Kenworthy P., and Wheeler, C. (2022) "Implications of the war in Ukraine for the global economy". EFI Policy Note 3, World Bank, April.

comply with sanctions or adapt to price increases.[3] It is rather European markets in sectors critically dependent on inputs from Ukraine (steel, software, semiconductors, cars and heavy manufacturing) that have been the most affected. The members of the Eurasian Economic Union (Armenia, Belarus, Kazakhstan and Kyrgyzstan) and of the Commonwealth of Independent States have also been impacted by disruptions in US, Chinese and German value chains that rely on imports from Russia, notably in the machinery, transport equipment, agribusiness and electronics sectors.

The war in Ukraine, however, has a more decisive secondary effect on globalisation, because China's stance on the war accelerates the Sino-US systemic rivalry. The sealing of a "friendship without limit" between Xi and Putin on the eve on the invasion, and the disruption of economic links between Russia and Western countries after the outbreak of the war, led to a steep rise in trade between China and Russia. The Sino-Russian rapprochement has compelled the US to accelerate the decoupling of its technology supply chains from the Chinese factory and innovation hubs, despite overall bilateral merchandise trade between China and the US reaching a record $690.3 billion in 2022.[4] In addition to the increased tariffs imposed by Donald Trump on some Chinese imports, Joe Biden is hitting China with export controls, visa bans, disinvestment and licensing denials. The war is thus gradually amplifying geopolitical risks, with growing implications for global trade. Less confidence is also causing a decrease in global foreign direct investment.

Yet neither the pandemic nor the war caused deglobalisation. The trend is rather toward slowbalisation[5] – the slowdown in the growth of global trade and investment – marking a shift from a long phase of deepening global economic integration. In 2021 businesses were already engaged in contingency planning in order to diversify supply (the so-called "China plus one" strategy). These plans started being implemented in 2022 after the invasion of Ukraine. Yet the decoupling currently remains limited. It was rebranded by the US administration in spring 2023 as a derisking strategy covering the limited scope of dual-use technologies: in addition to bans on exports of US semiconductors to China since 7 October 2022, control over outbound investment to China, starting from 2024, will be

---

3   WTO (2023) "One year of war in Ukraine". Report, p. 12.
4   According to the 2023 data of the US Census Bureau.
5   The term "slowbalisation" was first used in 2015, by the Dutch writer Adjiedj Bakas, and was popularised by the 24 January 2019 edition of *The Economist*, entitled "Slowbalisation: the future of global commerce".

limited to the sectors of semiconductors, microelectronics, quantum information technologies and artificial intelligence (AI).

The state of play of global trade in early 2023 signalled a weakening of global demand. The World Bank expects a deceleration of global trade in the short term, from 4% growth in 2022 to only 1.6% in 2023.[6] Global gross domestic product (GDP) will decline to 1.7% in 2023, down from the 3% that was predicted for the year back in mid-2022. In this assessment, the recovery in services trade will not prevent the expected slowdown of overall global trade growth. All regions of the world will be affected by monetary policy tightening, aimed at containing high inflation, financial stress and the continued disruptions determined by Russia's invasion of Ukraine. However, geoeconomic measures driven by geopolitical incentives will be the main driver of the transformation of global trade and investment, as reducing risks related to interdependence now trumps win-win international cooperation.

The shaping factors of geoeconomic competition

The US and China are engaged in an enduring systemic rivalry. China's increasingly assertive behaviour, its massive investment in military capabilities, its willingness to revise the liberal international order and concerns about the relative decline of American power have all focused minds in Washington. The prospect of China succeeding in dethroning the US as the world's leading power, as suggested by China's economic trajectory over the past decade, has led Democrats and Republicans to converge on the goal of preserving the US's technological and economic edge. The outcome of the 2024 US presidential elections will not bend the determination of the US to curb China's technological power, even though it could significantly affect how Washington pursues this underlying goal.

Multiple factors will determine the form that the Sino-American rivalry will take and the risk of escalation, with a variable impact on geoeconomic fragmentation. Risks related to geopolitical instability and conflict loom large. The fate of Taiwan is a critical factor in this context. A Chinese takeover would trigger retaliatory measures ranging from sanctions to military intervention and have disastrous implications for global trade and investment. Nearly half of the world's container ships pass through the

---

6   World Bank (2023) "Global economic prospects". Report, January.

Formosa Strait and would be immediately disrupted.[7] Whether tensions around Taiwan will lead to war will depend on several variables, including China's own calculations, the evolution of the balance of military power in the region and broader strategic considerations by the contenders. There is much uncertainty about the means that Xi would use to take control of the island, but the timing could also be critical. Among the economic factors, US dependence on imports of advanced semiconductors will be a very important one, since the island produces 65% of the world's needs and 90% of the most advanced chips. The more vulnerable the US will be to China taking over Taiwan's production capacity, the more determined it will be to prevent that from happening. What is clear is that geopolitical risks will foster geoeconomic fragmentation, and that the economy will be the primary arena of systemic rivalry. From this standpoint, some key factors shaping the future of globalisation stand out.

The first factor will be the ability of the Chinese Communist Party (CCP) to reverse or mitigate the prospects of sluggish Chinese economic growth over the medium term,[8] as the US might in part calibrate its economic coercion according to this. A progressive deceleration of Chinese economic growth and, therefore, of its financial capacity to support technological innovation could lead the US to limit the scope of its now so-called derisking strategy to some dual-use technologies, whereas a meaningful rebound could lead the US to be more aggressive and to extend decoupling to additional technologies or sectors. The slight rebound of the Chinese economy after the strict zero-Covid policy is supported by the reopening of the service sector industries, notably tourism. But it cannot mitigate the fact that Xi's dual circulation strategy is struggling, with less confidence in the growth of domestic consumption. This strategy aims at increasing third-country dependence on Chinese production, while simultaneously reducing China's dependence on imports. China's goal of self-sufficiency requires greater reliance on domestic consumption and continued development of innovation and production capacity for strategic technologies. But the Chinese economy faces structural problems that are limiting consumption growth, including a persistent crisis in the real estate sector, financial instability, stalled productivity, political control restraining corporate profitability and investment, an aging population

---

7   During the first seven months of 2022, 48% of the world's container ships passed through the Formosa Strait. (Varley, K. (2022) "Taiwan tensions raise risks in one of busiest shipping lanes". *Bloomberg*, 2 August.)

8   Srinivasan, K., Helbling, T., and Peiris, S. J. (2023) "Asia's easing economic headwinds make way for stronger recovery". *IMF Blog*, February.

and high youth unemployment. The return of Chinese consumer confidence will therefore be an important benchmark to monitor.

A second factor is the US's ability to coordinate with partners. The US derisking strategy intends to cut China off from accessing know-how for dual-use advanced technologies. Cutting off access to US innovation capacity is not enough if China can alternatively access third countries' technologies, notably those coming from European countries, Japan, South Korea, Canada or Taiwan. Will the US call for friendshoring lead to a fully fledged coordinated strategy with reliable partners? Or will the 2024 US presidential elections increase the appetite for a more "America first" policy, leading to more unilateral initiatives that increase mistrust among the historical allies of the US, as with the adoption of the Inflation Reduction Act? Will the US use extraterritorial instruments to pressure third countries to align with the US goals? Limiting trade diversion by imposing secondary sanctions on third countries that use US technology or software to produce goods exported to China requires major human and financial resources. It could also spark an adverse reaction among third countries, which could be tempted to align with China. Albeit slowly, several countries in the Global South, and notably the BRICS,[9] are already engaging in a dedollarisation strategy to avoid being exposed to US pressures. The finance ministers of the countries of the ASEAN (Association of Southeast Asian Nations) plan to limit the use of the dollar in their trade flows.[10] The supremacy of the dollar will not be challenged soon, but this trend is raising concerns in Washington. A related point is that Western policies might paradoxically deliver more integration between China and Asian countries. A recent report by World Bank economists Aaditya Mattoo and Michele Ruta underlines that the Western derisking strategy based on diversification of supply is already leading countries in regions such as Southeast Asia to become more dependent on China: the more goods they assemble for export to the West, the more reliant they become on inputs from China.[11]

---

9   Brazil, Russia, India, China and South Africa, with six new members joining in 2024: Argentina, Egypt, Ethiopia, Iran, Saudi Arabia and the United Arab Emirates.

10   Devonshire-Ellis, C. (2023) "ASEAN finance ministers and central banks consider dropping US dollar, euro and yen, Indonesia calls for phasing out Visa and Mastercard". ASEAN Briefing, 29 March.

11   Freund, C., Mattoo, A., Mulabdic, A., et al. (2023) "Is US trade policy reshaping global supply chains?" Paper presented at the IMF Conference on Geoeconomic Fragmentation, May, p. 4.

A third shaping factor is China's response. China is already the country that has implemented the most export restrictions on critical minerals between 2009–2020.[12] How Xi will now respond to the American export restrictions and engage in economic statecraft or coercion to meet China's own strategic ends can limit or increase the risk of escalation between the two powers and the domino effect on global trade and investment. While reaching carbon neutrality is now a priority for developed economies, there is rising awareness that the global dependence on China for certain components of green technologies and for refining critical minerals represents a high risk. The EU and the US are now supporting the mass production of semiconductors and green technologies with massive public financial investment. But Xi could more aggressively leverage China's monopoly position in the production of some components of these technologies. There are already worrying signals that export restrictions could be applied on several components, such as polysilicon and wafers for solar panels, refining technologies,[13] and alloy tech for making high-performance magnets derived from rare earths (which are critical components in wind turbines and electric vehicle batteries), as well as more recently on gallium and germanium used in defence technologies. The objective may be not only to preserve the dominance of Chinese production by avoiding the outflow of Chinese investment to those third countries willing to produce these same green technologies, but also economic coercion. It will take time to move away from heavy reliance on China, and Xi may not be willing to give the necessary time to strategic rivals.

A fourth shaping factor is the reaction of third countries. Efforts to isolate Russia have not succeeded in the so-called Global South. Perceived as a cause of global socioeconomic instability, the war reinforces a postcolonial discourse on the South's own interests in relation to the Western bloc. Nor do countries in the South want to alienate Russia's closest partner, China, which for many of them has become their main trading partner. Their capacity to navigate between the blocs will be challenged and could lead some countries to choose a side. The EU is not immune to this need for complex navigation. How Europeans unite around a clear strategy towards China will be decisive if they are faced with economic coercion. The focus is currently on risk reduction, not decoupling from

---

12   Kowalski, P., and Legendre, C. (2023) "Raw materials critical for the green transition: production, international trade and export restrictions". Policy Paper 269, OECD, April.

13   Tabeta, S. (2023) "China weighs export ban for rare-earth magnet tech". *Nikkei Asia*, 6 April.

the Chinese market. But China, as much as the US, may not leave them enough time or leeway for an orderly derisking strategy. Europeans may be forced to adapt to the initiatives of US and China.

A fifth shaping factor is the erosion of the international rules-based order, and specifically decreasing conformity to the World Trade Organization (WTO) rules. The distortive practices of China, such as unlimited subsidies for state-owned enterprises, have already led to unfair competition. Since 2019 the US has been blocking the appellate body of the WTO's dispute settlement mechanism by opposing the nomination of new judges. The local content provisions included in the 2022 US Inflation Reduction Act are not compatible with the WTO's nondiscrimination principle and risk disincentivising others from abiding by this rule. Many third countries believe that this return to a power-based system makes them more vulnerable, but it is unclear whether they carry enough weight to steer the course in a different direction. Falling back on trade protectionism as a short-term fix would have a negative impact on global trade, stability and prosperity.

All these factors will interact, with reciprocal amplification effects. They have the potential to shift the prospects for the global trade order from some sort of orderly reconfiguration to various forms of fragmentation.

Different shades of fragmentation of global trade and investment

At the time of writing these scenarios, there is little likelihood that an end to the war in Ukraine will be achieved quickly, or that the Sino-American rivalry will subside in the short term. There is very low probability for a cooperative scenario in which China and the United States prioritise global prosperity over national economic interests, engaging in the protection of public goods (climate, health, the environment) and supporting an open world trade system with more multilateral rules.

The International Monetary Fund (IMF) has instead focused on estimates of the long-term cost of trade fragmentation, which could range from a decrease of 0.2% in global output in a limited fragmentation scenario to an almost 7% drop in a severe scenario.[14] Some countries could be particularly exposed to technological decoupling, with a risk of losing up to 12% of their GDP. The three scenarios proposed below present different degrees of fragmentation.

---

14 Georgieva, K. (2023) "Confronting fragmentation where it matters most: trade, debt, and climate action". *IMF Blog*, January.

Scenario 1: managed coexistence

This first scenario is based on a Chinese economic progressive slowdown. Xi's focus on state-owned enterprises, despite their low productivity and the CCP's increasing control over the private sector, limits China's innovation capacity. Stagnating domestic demand requires preserving access to external demand. Xi avoids adopting protectionist measures that could be reciprocated and thus limit access to strategic foreign markets for Chinese exports. However, China's leadership in some key technologies (AI, supercomputing) allows it to promote its own regulations.

The US limits the decoupling of the US and Chinese technology ecosystems to dual-use technologies. Broad economic interdependence remains strong for daily consumption goods. The massive public support provided to US companies allows the country to progressively increase its production capacity for green technologies and to reduce its dependence on Chinese technologies. The US actively invests in setting the rules for new technologies such as AI and biotech.

This scenario of limited rivalry is determined by the fact that neither China nor the US can afford the cost of a broader decoupling. The coexistence of two blocs is illustrated by the development of two sets of regulations for new technologies, with third countries having the option to produce in or for those big markets.

Xi's interest in keeping global markets open leads him to support a functioning WTO. However, the US is not coming back to the negotiating table, and the organisation survives merely as a discussion forum. The US actively seeks to promote a new world order "minus China" based on the regulation of new technologies. Washington adopts a cooperative approach with key reliable countries, which leads to more friendshoring and a regionalisation of supply chains based on geopolitical criteria. This cooperative approach allows for further transatlantic rapprochement. The EU itself expands its industrial and innovation strategy beyond the green technologies sector and promotes its own regulatory approach to new technologies (as with the currently proposed European AI Act). The US and EU struggle to overcome their discrepancies over the protection of private data and more broadly the new ecosystem of technology regulations. Yet, together with additional partners, they succeed in launching plurilateral (or "minilateral") initiatives, which remain open to additional members of the WTO.

A large bloc of nonaligned countries continues to navigate between competitive regulatory spaces and joint plurilateral initiatives on an ad hoc basis. Yet, in accordance with the "gravity effect" of geographical proximity on trade, increasing economic integration in Southeast Asia leads the countries of the region to progressively increase their dependence on China.

Scenario 2: disordered fragmentation

More CCP control over the private sector does not prevent China from receiving more foreign direct investment in high-quality sectors (advanced manufacturing, higher-quality services, high tech, energy conservation and environmental protection). Persistently sluggish global demand makes the Chinese market and innovation hubs even more attractive for foreign companies. In addition, Xi uses the leverage of existing high dependence on Chinese components to raise their prices. Foreign companies are therefore encouraged to produce in China and export to their home market rather than import expensive Chinese components and produce in their home market. The outbound investment control measures adopted by the US and the EU are limited to sectors of dual-use technologies and leave much room for foreign investment. China's growth benefits from greater flows of foreign direct investment. The conservative growth estimates of the past are contradicted by an economic rebound, while China's ability to substitute imports with Chinese technology grows.

Despite rising voices warning against the cost of deeper global fragmentation, Congress pressures the US administration to focus on economic security and to adopt a more aggressive "America first" policy, further breaching the WTO's nondiscrimination rule. The focus is more than ever on an aggressive industrial policy (with a subsidy race and local content requirements), which makes coordination with partners difficult.

There is an escalation in retaliation between the US and China, as the latter moves from raising the export prices of components and strategic minerals to introducing export restrictions on them. The escalation of economic coercion is not limited to the technology sector and tends to create structural inflation throughout many sectors.

This has a domino effect on third countries, with less incentives to conform to multilateral rules. The dismantlement of the rules-based order generates instability and a disordered diversification of trade routes, with numerous supply disruptions. There is an increased risk of trade conflicts.

The alignment of countries from the Global South with the US or China also depends on the security guarantees provided by each power. The countries of Southeast Asia fail to mitigate this disordered fragmentation of global trade with more regional integration. Only sectoral plurilateral agreements – bringing together a very limited number of countries – survive or develop, such as the Digital Economy Partnership Agreement (DEPA) between Singapore, Chile and New Zealand.

Scenario 3: invasion of Taiwan and unravelling of globalisation

It is unclear how the US and the rest of the world would ultimately respond to an escalation of tensions around Taiwan. Much would depend on the modalities of this escalation: that is, Chinese economic embargo or military aggression. While a progressive embargo of Taiwan would allow the US and allies to impose calibrated economic sanctions on China, a military aggression might call for military support for Taiwan. The timing of this crisis would be another critical factor, since the amount of advanced semiconductor production capacity that the US will have achieved by then may have a strong impact on the calibration of retaliatory measures. Taiwan currently manufactures 65% of the world's semiconductors and more than 90% of the most advanced chips; 65% of the world's goods exports depend on semiconductors, including 5% consisting of the semiconductors themselves, 29% of the goods that contain them and 30% of the goods whose manufacturing depends on them.[15]

If the US had time to reduce its dependence on Taiwanese semiconductors, future administrations or Congress might be more reluctant to bear the high cost of unconditional support for Taiwan. If, however, that was not the case, then the Chinese takeover of Taiwan would empower Beijing to restrict or ban access to Taiwanese semiconductors. This would have an immediate negative impact on global supply chains and all related downstream industries. Arguably, the Chinese economy itself would be so badly affected by the resulting global recession that Xi would have no interest in stopping the exports of Taiwanese semiconductors completely. But China could raise prices or condition access to these semiconductors, causing shortages and major domino effects on all companies that do not have enough stocks. This would also mean imposing

---

15   Asian Development Bank (2022) "Asian economic integration report 2022". February, p. 22.

a ceiling on American technological innovation, while China accelerates its pace of innovation. Beijing may also extend China's influence over other third countries if they want to access this strategic technology. An erosion of American economic power and the strengthening of China's would usher in a long-term shift to a unipolar world led by China.

In the case of conflict over Taiwan, third countries would be forced to quickly rally to one bloc or the other. The new alliances would cause the suspension of the preferential conditions of some free trade agreements. It is difficult to imagine what kind of world order would emerge from what would turn out to be a third World War, except perhaps that the EU would fully join forces with the US. The regional integration within the two trade blocs would deepen. The disaster of a war provoked by the great powers might also lead to stronger integration among the middle powers of the so-called Global South.

Is the EU well equipped to navigate a fragmented global trade environment?

On 30 March 2023, the president of the European Commission, Ursula von der Leyen, stated that the EU would prioritise derisking – reducing the risks associated with excessive dependence – over decoupling from China. Bringing the member states and the business sector to converge on the same risk assessment is thus the first aim of the economic security strategy proposed by the Commission on 20 June, which sought to speed the coordination of member states in a situation where their national competences are at stake.

While the single market is threatened by a return of economic nationalism as much as global trade is, it remains Europeans' main asset in reducing excessive dependence and needs to be consolidated. The important public financial support required to develop the entire value chain of green and disruptive technologies and decrease dependence on non-European suppliers can hardly be supported by individual countries. The challenge for the 27 is thus to preserve a level playing field within the single market while focusing on strengthening the pooling of their capacities.

The European Union also has its own interests and specific constraints. It is more dependent on external demand than the US. The ratio of exports to GDP was 8% for the US in 2019, compared with 15% for the EU. It is also more integrated into the Chinese economy than the US is. Furthermore, security is a competence of the member states. While the

G7 members decided to coordinate for "greater economic resilience and economic security" at the Hiroshima summit on 30 May 2023, the Europeans intend to develop their own derisking doctrine to avoid simply falling into line. The United States has given up on opening up its markets, in favour of reindustrialising the country through massive public investment. Europe, on the other hand, is adopting an industrial policy while at the same time continuing to rely on trade, which is even more necessary since the supply of certain raw materials has become strategically important for green and digital technologies. While Washington frees itself from multilateral rules, Brussels defends the reinforcement of a system of fair competition. For Europeans, the challenge remains to adopt a security strategy for an open economy.

The economic security strategy proposed by the European Commission thus aims to accelerate the implementation of several recent initiatives ranging from industrial capacity building (the Chips Act, the Net-Zero Industry Act and the Critical Raw Materials Act) to greater protection (autonomous trade defence instruments, such as control of foreign direct investment and foreign subsidies; reciprocity on public procurement and anticoercion instruments; protection of critical infrastructures; promotion of European standards; cybersecurity measures; protection of 5G infrastructures; and scientific cooperation guidelines). Added to this is cooperation with partner countries to secure strategic supplies. The larger purpose is not only bringing coherence between those initiatives to increase the resilience of value chains but limiting the development of systemic rivals' military capacities. Planning an update to the list of dual-use technologies banned from exports, which could now also be excluded from outbound investment to China and other countries of concern in order to limit technology transfers, shows that Europeans are seriously considering the risk of disorderly or conflictual fragmentation of the global economy.

The short-term deadlines set by the Commission for a common assessment of the risks that Europe faces at the European Council of December 2023 underline the urgent need for strong cohesion among Europeans, and ultimately the importance of increasing the European Union's own resources to invest in innovation capabilities that are up to the challenges.

Annalisa Prizzon

6 | A growing gap between development cooperation and development needs

At the mid-point towards the 2030 Sustainable Development Goals (SDGs) signed in 2015, the overall picture of their implementation looks bleak. Even before the Covid-19 pandemic, the progress that did occur was not at the pace needed for truly transformative change.[1] In 2022 the Russian full-scale invasion of Ukraine directly or indirectly led to spikes in energy and food prices, rising inflation, greater costs of financing, unsustainable debt and additional pressure on government budgets. The confluence of all these crises is now slowing down progress on Agenda 2030 and even leading to setbacks – for example, for the goal of eradicating extreme poverty.[2] Calls to "rescue" the SDGs are mounting.

Development cooperation is not a sufficient condition for sustainable growth and development, but it is necessary to finance public expenditure and investment in order to foster economic growth. Over the coming years, development partners will, however, face tougher choices about their competing foreign policy objectives and the allocation of their increasingly tight public finances, against a background of the mounting needs of low- and middle-income countries.

This chapter first analyses whether and how the volumes and allocation of development cooperation will be affected by the war in Ukraine. It then highlights the main issues and actors that will drive change, sketches potential patterns of change for development cooperation and summarises what this all means for policymakers in Europe.

---

1   United Nations (2019) "Report of the Secretary-General on SDG progress 2019: special edition". Report, UN (https://sustainabledevelopment.un.org/content/documents/24978Report_of_the_SG_on_SDG_Progress_2019.pdf).
2   United Nations (2022) "The Sustainable Development Goals report 2022". Report, UN (https://unstats.un.org/sdgs/report/2022/).

How the war in Ukraine affects development finance

Increased development assistance for Ukraine and for in-donor refugee costs, with a potential crowding-out effect for other countries and sectors

Russia's full-scale invasion of Ukraine showed that G7 countries and multilateral organisations can react quickly and significantly in the face of an emergency, scaling up humanitarian assistance and development cooperation programmes, either in Ukraine or supporting displaced Ukrainian citizens in donor countries.

Concerning bilateral support, the Kiel Institute for the World Economy has kept track of the military, financial and humanitarian aid commitments from 40 governments and the EU institutions for Ukraine in the context of the war – a total of $143 billion between January 2022 and January 2023.[3] As a comparison, total official development assistance (ODA) reached the $200 billion mark over the same period across all countries and sectors. In terms of volume, the United States is the single largest bilateral supporter of Ukraine so far, counting for half of the commitments, followed by the EU institutions, the United Kingdom and Germany.

As to multilateral partners, the International Monetary Fund (IMF), the World Bank, the European Bank for Reconstruction and Development (EBRD) and the European Investment Bank (EIB) significantly and quickly expanded their assistance to Ukraine, which amounts to a substantial proportion of their portfolios. The IMF approved a new programme for Ukraine in record time after the start of the war.[4] As of April 2023, the World Bank has mobilised more than $23 billion in financial support to Ukraine.[5] This is a considerable figure, as the total commitments of

---

3   Trebesch, C., Antezza, A., Bushnell, K., et al. (2023) "The Ukraine support tracker: which countries help Ukraine and how?" Working Paper 2218, Kiel Institute for the World Economy, February (https://www.ifw-kiel.de/publications/kiel-working-papers/2022/the-ukraine-support-tracker-which-countries-help-ukraine-and-how-17204/).

4   IMF (2022) "IMF executive board approves US$15.6 billion under a new Extended Fund Facility (EFF) arrangement for Ukraine as part of a US$115 billion overall support package". Press Release 23/101, IMF (https://www.imf.org/en/News/Articles/2023/03/31/pr23101-ukraine-imf-executive-board-approves-usd-billion-new-eff-part-of-overall-support-package).

5   World Bank (2023) "World Bank Group financing support mobilization to Ukraine since February 24". Brief, World Bank, 29 June (https://www.worldbank.org/en/country/ukraine/brief/world-bank-emergency-financing-package-for-ukraine).

the entire World Bank Group in a year are about $105 billion.[6] The EBRD agreed to invest up to $3 billion between 2022 and 2023 (the EBRD's annual investment is about $10 billion). The EIB has mobilised and disbursed €1.7 billion since the start of the invasion.

But the rapid response of bilateral and multilateral organisations came at a price. First, it crowded out resources for existing development commitments and lower-income countries. Annual official development assistance (ODA) kept rising in 2022, seeing a 13.6% increase.[7] Annual ODA growth in 2022 was also among the highest ever recorded, second only to 2005, when exceptional debt relief packages were agreed upon at the G8 summit in Gleneagles. At a closer scrutiny, however, if in-donor refugee costs were taken out of the ODA figures, then across the members of the Development Assistance Committee of the Organisation for Economic Co-operation and Development (OECD) the increase in ODA in 2022 would be much smaller: 4.6%. Besides, when taking ODA flows to Ukraine out of the total figure, in 2022 ODA to objectives and countries other than Ukraine dropped by more than 4% compared with 2021.[8] Some donors, such as the UK, froze nonessential ODA spending for some time,[9] and others, such as Denmark and Sweden, cut other components of their ODA budgets.[10] On the multilateral front, the EBRD delayed the start of the expansion of its operations to sub-Saharan Africa.[11]

Second, the changing patterns of development spending carried a political cost. The trust of African leaders in Western countries has eroded even further. The rapid response to the war in Ukraine clashes with a slow reaction to juxtaposed crises that have received little financial attention from donor countries (such as famine in the Horn of Africa,

---

6   World Bank (2022) "Fiscal year data". World Bank website (https://www.worldbank.org/en/about/annual-report/fiscal-year-data).

7   OECD (2023) "ODA levels in 2022: preliminary data". Detailed summary note, OECD, Paris (https://www.oecd.org/dac/financing-sustainable-development/ODA-2022-summary.pdf).

8   Prizzon, A., and Getzel, B. (2023) "Prospects for aid in 2023: a watershed moment or business as usual?" ODI Insight, 18 April (https://odi.org/en/insights/prospects-for-aid-in-2023-watershed-moment-or-business-as-usual/).

9   "Inquiry on the future of UK aid". International Development Committee, UK Parliament website (https://committees.parliament.uk/work/940/future-of-uk-aid/).

10   Prizzon, A. (2022) "What prospects for aid in 2022 (and beyond)?" ODI Insight, 30 June (https://odi.org/en/insights/what-prospects-for-aid-in-2022-and-beyond/).

11   Bains, M., and Prizzon, A. (2022) "Five issues for the EBRD to consider in its expansion to sub-Saharan Africa". ODI Insight, 7 June (https://odi.org/en/insights/five-issues-for-the-ebrd-to-consider-in-its-expansion-to-sub-saharan-africa/).

food security, rising energy prices and even higher inflation than usual in many countries). Many African leaders openly said they felt increasingly left behind and overlooked the longer the war in Ukraine continued.[12]

More intense discussion on the reform of the international financial system

In 2022 the finances and policies of multilateral development banks (MDBs) gained centre stage in the debates on financing for development. Most of their shareholders had very limited wiggle room in their international development cooperation budgets, as they were attempting to balance the books after the public spending spree brought on by the Covid-19 pandemic, and many European donors were having to find space in their budgets to cover the costs associated with refugees fleeing to their countries.

The scale and length of the Covid-19 pandemic and the growing pressure to deal with the impact of climate change were also stark reminders that global challenges need global solutions and coordination. MDBs are perceived to be well placed to work on these issues because of their global or regional reach. They can leverage their balance sheets and put in place a much quicker countercyclical response to crises than individual governments, as shown by the response to the war in Ukraine.

Current trends, however, challenge the ability of MDBs to scale up development finance. Bilateral donors are increasingly delivering their programmes and projects directly, as opposed to via multilateral channels, according to the preliminary ODA figures for 2022.[13] At the same time, these donors are putting increasing pressure on MDB management to define and implement a much more ambitious agenda but with the same amount of resources. Several parallel policy processes will keep attention on the MDB reform agenda high in 2023 and beyond: the Evolution Roadmap (World Bank Group); a strong commitment to strengthening MDBs in the Leaders' Declaration of India's G20 presidency; and the Paris "Summit for a New Global Financing Pact" in June.

---

12   Kende-Robb, C. (2022) "A crisis is coming: 4 steps to address Africa's urgent financing needs". *Agenda* blog, World Economic Forum (https://www.weforum.org/agenda/2022/08/four-steps-to-address-africa-s-urgent-financing-needs/).

13   OECD (2023) "ODA Levels in 2022".

More lower-income countries at risk of future debt crises

As a result of slower growth and higher borrowing to deal with the aftermath of the Covid-19 crisis, falling tax receipts, expanding social programmes to help address the consequences of rising food and energy prices, and looming interest payments on sovereign bonds, many more countries are facing an increasing risk of debt distress. In 2022, Sri Lanka defaulted on its debt, and Pakistan averted default only because of to a timely IMF programme.

This is not yet a systemic crisis comparable to those in the 1990s and 2000s, but difficulties in debt repayments are now rising in a significant number of countries. Out of the 35 low-income countries in sub-Saharan Africa, 19 are in debt distress or facing a high risk of debt distress.[14] Borrowing from capital markets is becoming more and more expensive, unaffordable or even impossible for countries without a good credit rating.

In previous debt crises, bilateral and multilateral donors were criticised for doing "too little, too late" to address the rising debt burden in lower-income countries. To balance the books, official donors – bilateral and multilateral – need to offset the debt cancellation, and that comes out of the aid budget. This is a difficult ask right now, at a time when budgets are under considerable strain.

Countries can default on their debt, but doing so limits access to new financial resources and long-term credibility in international capital markets. At the same time, lending from China to low- and middle-income countries has been falling,[15] with a rising share of nonperforming loans that will likely affect future Chinese operations overseas.[16]

Growing needs, tough choices

Future trajectories of development cooperation will be affected by several factors and actors. Four of them stand out because they have

---

14   IMF (2023) "Sub-Saharan Africa regional economic outlook". Report, IMF, April (https://www.imf.org/en/Publications/REO/SSA/Issues/2023/04/14/regional-economic-outlook-for-sub-saharan-africa-april-2023).

15   Ray, R., and Simmons, B. A (2020) "Tracking China's overseas development finance". Boston University website, 7 December (https://www.bu.edu/gdp/2020/12/07/tracking-chinas-overseas-development-finance/).

16   Kynge, J. (2023) "China hit by surge in Belt and Road bad loans". *Financial Times*, 16 April.

either direct or indirect consequences for the volumes, access to and allocation of development finance. These four factors are the speed at which Western economies will leave the high-inflation/low-growth trap, the ability to tap into alternative funding sources other than ODA for development cooperation, China's role in development cooperation, and the long-standing question of who is to pay for climate adaptation and a low-carbon transition.

Growth prospects of Western economies

In the immediate aftermath of severe financial and economic crises, development cooperation budgets tend to be countercyclical – that is, they grow while economies shrink.[17] However, aid budgets are currently suffering from cuts as crises prolong and deepen. Most Western governments are trying to balance the books after launching vast social spending programmes and subsidies to cope with the impact of the pandemic and the war in Ukraine. The sooner significant and sustained economic growth will resume in Western economies, the quicker public finances will be restored and the space to expand development cooperation budgets increased. Though energy prices are falling, inflation remains high, and so are the expectations for interest rates, undermining the impact of large-scale public investment on long-term growth in both the US and Europe.

Ability to tap into alternative financing sources other than development cooperation

While annual ODA passed the $200 billion mark in 2022, this is a drop in the ocean compared with the financing needs of low and middle-income countries, estimated at $1 trillion per year.[18] Achieving a rise in finance for development might require drawing on other headings in government budgets, such as defence or climate finance. This points to growing competition for public funding, at a time when governments are under pressure to expand defence spending too. Other options include channelling

---

17   Carson, L., Schäfer, M. S., Prizzon, A., et al. (2021) "Prospects for aid at times of crisis". Working paper 606, ODI, March (https://odi.org/en/publications/prospects-for-aid-at-times-of-crisis/).

18   Songwe, V., Stern, N., and Bhattacharya, A. (2022) "Finance for climate action: scaling up investment for climate and development". Report of the Independent High-Level Expert Group on Climate Finance, November (https://www.lse.ac.uk/granthaminstitute/wp-content/uploads/2022/11/IHLEG-Finance-for-Climate-Action-1.pdf).

proceeds from cross-border financial transaction taxes or carbon border adjustment mechanisms, as proposed under the Bridgetown Agenda, or redirecting a share of proceeds from donor-country carbon markets or carbon taxes.[19] There is scope for progress on other fronts too, such as making better use of existing MDB capital;[20] increasing MDB capital, as it offers good value for money for shareholders;[21] and finally the more effective mobilisation of private capital – a long-standing challenge, especially in low-income countries.[22]

China's role in development cooperation

China will be one of the main actors shaping the future of development cooperation. From the mid-2000s onwards it was one of the largest providers of development finance – until 2017, external lending by the China Development Bank exceeded that of the World Bank.[23] But since 2016, China has drastically reduced its foreign lending programme for both concessional and nonconcessional loans, a move associated with slowing economic growth and nonperforming loans, as mentioned above. Falling overseas lending from China will have implications for the position of many developing countries when negotiating sources of finance with traditional donors, because it will reduce their options.[24] Countries used to turn down loans from bilateral and multilateral donors if they were not aligned with government priorities or if they were too

---

19   Lankes, H. P., and Prizzon, A. (2023) "Multilateral development bank reform can – and must – benefit both low- and middle-income countries". ODI Insight, 13 April (https://odi.org/en/insights/multilateral-development-bank-reform-can-and-must-benefit-both-low-and-middle-income-countries/).

20   G20 expert panel on the review of capital adequacy frameworks (2022) "Boosting MDBs' investing capacity". Report, October (https://www.dt.mef.gov.it/export/sites/sitodt/modules/documenti_it/news/news/CAF-Review-Report.pdf).

21   Humphrey, C., and Prizzon, A. (2020) "Scaling up multilateral bank finance for the Covid-19 recovery". ODI Insight (https://odi.org/en/insights/scaling-up-multilateral-bank-finance-for-the-covid-19-recovery/).

22   Attridge, S., and Gouett, M. (2021) "Development finance institutions: the need for bold action to invest better". Report, ODI, April (https://odi.org/en/publications/development-finance-institutions-the-need-for-bold-action-to-invest-better/).

23   Ray, R., and Simmons, B. A (2020) "Tracking China's overseas development finance".

24   Prizzon, A., Greenhill, R., and Mustapha, S. (2016) "An age of choice for development finance: evidence from country case studies". Report, ODI, April (https://odi.org/en/publications/an-age-of-choice-for-development-finance-evidence-from-country-case-studies/).

slow to negotiate.[25] China is also creating a stumbling block for debt renegotiations, even though the picture seems to be improving at the time of writing. The position of Chinese authorities is likely to evolve as they better understand that the involvement of MDBs in debt cancellation will mean lower lending volumes (since MDB resources will have to be used to compensate for unpaid loans rather than issuing new loans) and as the number of countries close to default rises.

Who is going to pay for climate adaptation and mitigation?

Pressure is growing to meet the $100 billion international climate finance commitments, as bilateral donors are still falling short of it. Recipient countries are not willing to take up loans intended to build resilience and adapt to the consequences of climate change – a problem that they stress they have not created or significantly contributed to.[26] However, grant financing remains a scarce resource and it is unlikely to grow significantly in the medium term.

Looking ahead: geopolitics overshadowing development

Falling levels of development cooperation and fewer financing options put Agenda 2030 at risk even further

A primary objective of development cooperation is to help eradicate poverty and promote growth and development in beneficiary countries. But with rising geopolitical tensions and a multipolar world, it is likely that development cooperation will increasingly be used as a tool for foreign policy and commercial goals. Less focused on poverty eradication, funding would progressively target cooperation on science and technology and on trade facilitation, to take two examples.

The "age of choice"[27] for development finance – that is, countries being able to access not just traditional development cooperation funds, but also lending from China and international capital markets – might be coming to an end. Development cooperation may become once again the

---

25   Ibid.
26   Prizzon, A., Josten, M., and Gyuzalyan, H. (2022) "Country perspectives on multilateral development banks: a survey analysis". Report, ODI, April (https://odi.org/en/publications/country-perspectives-on-multilateral-development-banks-a-survey-analysis/).
27   Prizzon, A., Greenhill, R., and Mustapha, S. (2016) "An age of choice".

main source of external finance, as access to capital markets becomes increasingly expensive or no longer possible and Chinese overseas lending falls significantly. While development cooperation is not sufficient for growth and development, it is a necessary condition to enable public spending and investment. Moreover, without a large scale-up of resources, an already struggling Agenda 2030 might become even more unlikely to be achieved, as would international climate finance commitments.

At the same time, many Western leaders have stepped up their initiatives and visits to Africa to counteract the rising influence of Russia in the region or nonalignment over the war in Ukraine. This is also partly in response to the rising "crisis of trust" – that is, African leaders' diminishing trust in G7 countries, a challenge that well preceded the war.[28]

Geopolitical tensions may also compromise the success of the reform agenda of international financial institutions and reduce the role of multilateral aid

The discussion on MDB reform has become increasingly technical. So far it has focused on reshaping the vision and mandate of these institutions, as well as changing their operational models and expanding their lending capacity, particularly for the World Bank. But the composition and governance structures of MDBs are an inherently political question. Negotiations might be simplified by setting aside contentious requests from emerging economies (particularly China) for the modification of governance structures and voting rights. However, not tackling these requests at the same time as the reform of mandates and operations will likely jeopardise the full and long-term implementation of technical reforms. Furthermore, as many shareholders increasingly use bilateral aid channels, the ambitious reform of multilateral development banks might not have enough financial backing, which could point to a proportionally smaller role for multilateral organisations in international development.

Many lower-income countries might have to deal with another round of debt crises

Official bilateral and multilateral creditors will need to act quickly – and it will be more expensive – if the situation escalates. The number of lower-income countries in debt distress or at high risk of distress remains high,

---

28 Signé, L. (2021) "How to restore US credibility in Africa". *Foreign Policy*, 15 January.

but progress on debt restructuring modalities is slow. This crisis is less systemic than those in the 1990s and 2000s, but this time it coincides with economic slowdown in many Western countries rather than booming economies, which makes relief efforts more unlikely. Development partners are likely to wait until many more countries are on the brink of debt default before acting. However, just as in the previous debt crises, addressing the impact of the crises rather than their root causes will be far more expensive for development partners and MDBs.

Policy implications and priorities for the EU and EU member states

The war in Ukraine has triggered several knock-on effects for development cooperation: first, the rapid mobilisation of resources for the development and humanitarian crises in Ukraine; second, mounting needs for many low- and middle-income countries facing rising food and energy prices, while already trying to balance the books in the aftermath of the Covid-19 crisis; and, finally, greater competition for scarce resources. At the same time, development partners – bilateral donors, the EU and MDBs – all face shrinking or just-about-stable budgets for international cooperation. The reality is that, for the foreseeable future, development partners will not be in a position – both financially and politically – to spend and invest more in development cooperation programmes abroad. But there are some options to make the most of the existing budgets and allocate them more efficiently.

First, more development cooperation should be spent and invested in beneficiary countries to help rescue the SDGs. Country programmable aid (CPA) – the core component of ODA spent in each country – fell marginally from $64.1 billion in 2020 to $61.4 billion in 2021 in real terms, despite total ODA going up. Pending final data, a further decline in CPA in 2022 is widely expected. Following the exceptional investment for supporting displaced Ukrainians in Europe in 2022, it is time to turn the tide and spend more on developing countries rather than donor countries.

Second, solutions are needed to deal with the debt crisis, including debt relief and debt restructuring. As debt distress mounts in many countries, bilateral and multilateral development partners should prepare for a new wave of debt relief packages. The IMF is already calling for "another Gleneagles-like moment".

Finally, EU member states need a stronger commitment to MDB reform. The evidence for investing in the multilateral development banking system is compelling, all the more so as development cooperation budgets are under pressure. First, MDBs offer very good value for money. For example, the World Bank's International Bank for Reconstruction and Development (IBRD) window had lent over $700 billion and generated $55 billion in net income by 2018, based on shareholder capital of only $16.5 billion – 46 times leverage, compared with between 0.3 and 22 times for blended finance.[29] The total paid-in capital to the IBRD since 1944 represents about 10% of aid disbursements in just one year. Second, channelling resources through MDBs would strengthen the case that the EU supports multilateralism that delivers. Third, MDBs can provide the type of risky long-term investments needed to support structural changes in economies in a way that commercial banks or capital markets might avoid. Lastly, multilateral development organisations score better than bilateral donors in the development effectiveness agenda, especially in terms of alignment with national priorities and policy engagement. Recipient-country governments prefer working with multilateral organisations over bilateral donors. Multilateral actors are also perceived as more trustworthy, flexible and responsive and as having valuable technical skills and policy expertise.

---

29 Humphrey, C., and Prizzon, A. (2020) "Scaling up multilateral bank finance".

Daniela Schwarzer

7 | The EU put to the test: fast forward, catching up or lagging behind?

When Russia started the full-scale invasion of Ukraine in 2022, the European Union had already been handling one and a half decades of crises. The EU has been confronted with multiple challenges, internal and external, since the financial crisis spilled into Europe in 2007–2008 and the sovereign debt and banking crisis starting in 2010 challenged the existence of the monetary union.

Each crisis, albeit to different degrees, simultaneously strengthened centrifugal and centripetal forces in Europe. On the one hand, the crisis in the eurozone, the annexation of Crimea and the war in Ukraine's east that Russia started in 2014, the migration crisis of 2015, Brexit, and finally the Covid pandemic all challenged the practical functioning of the EU, political decision-making and cohesion. On several occasions, governments initially chose purely national responses to trans-European problems, out of domestic pressure or because the EU did not provide effective tools to react to an acute challenge. This endangered European integration, while actors critical of the EU seized on the situation to make anti-EU arguments.[1]

On the other hand, most governments later self-corrected initial actions, in particular those measures that undermined the principles and freedoms of movement on which the EU is built. Policymakers designed new policies or even institutions to cope with the acute problems. They put in place new financial tools to fund European responses in previously underdeveloped areas of integration, which over time improved the EU's capacity to act. Consequently, every single crisis over the past 15 years

---

1   For an analysis of the drivers of integration and disintegration in the context of 15 years of crises for the EU, see Schwarzer, D. (2021) *Final Call. Wie Europa sich zwischen China und den USA behaupten kann* (Frankfurt am Main: Campus Verlag), Chapter 2, pp. 59–129.

has strengthened the EU while also heightening the internal tensions that need to be reckoned with when the next crisis arises.

Russia's brutal attempt to erase Ukraine from the map as a sovereign state is this decade's most consequential event on the European continent so far. Despite internal divisions over its relationship with Russia, the European Union has developed European policy responses, ranging from sanctions to support for arms deliveries and to a new, more cautious economic security approach. But the longer the war lasts, the more fragile joint European positions may get. Additionally, the big questions around the design of the European Union are back on the table, with the new dynamics in the enlargement process (which has been extended to Ukraine and Moldova), the creation of the European Political Community and a new debate on deepening or differentiating the European Union.

This chapter first assesses the continuity and discontinuity that the war has brought, focusing not only on policy issues but also on the pressures to redesign the European order beyond the EU. It discusses factors of change and explores potential future developments within the EU and across the Atlantic. It concludes with recommendations for policy-making and institutional reform, as the shattered European security order needs to be met with ambitious thinking about the future of European cooperation and integration on a continental scale.

Redrawing Europe's map

In 2022 and 2023, as a direct response to Russia's large-scale invasion of Ukraine, the EU took measures that would have been unthinkable a year or two earlier on the economic, military and humanitarian fronts. But, for the EU, the most important implication of this war is the collapse of the cooperative post-Cold War security order, which had already featured deep and visible cracks at least since Russia's annexation of Crimea and its interventions in the Donbas. Russia's latest aggression has pushed EU member states to rethink defence and energy security nationally but also in the EU context, ushering in a redefinition of security, stability and cooperation on a continental scale. The war has moreover deepened the economic crisis that Europe was still coping with due to Covid. Given the war's global repercussions, it has pushed the EU and its member states to review their relationship with other regions and countries. Finally, it has increased pressures on national and European democracies to improve their capacity to meet citizens' expectations, increase resilience and innovate.

The shattered European security order

Russia has brutally violated the principles of the European security order that the Soviet Union and later Russia negotiated with US and European leaders during the Cold War and the post-Cold War era. For a long time, the assumption prevailed that an imperialist attack triggering a full-scale interstate war would no longer happen in Europe. During the Cold War, the adversaries of the time agreed on ground rules to make an escalation of the East–West conflict less likely. The basic rules of the European peace order were further developed after 1989, such as with the 1990 Charter of Paris and later the 1997 NATO–Russia Founding Act. None of these agreements today provides a credible base for security on the European continent anymore, and it is now a top priority for Europeans and their allies – most notably the US and Canada – to prepare the ground for a new approach, which, for the time being, cannot be a cooperative one that includes Russia. Moscow started departing years ago from the framework designed to preserve security in Europe. Russia has made repeated interventions by force in its neighbourhood to secure and expand its sphere of influence or to prevent the disintegration of its own state, including the aggression against Georgia in 2008 and against Ukraine in 2014. It has also explicitly called for a renegotiation of the European security order.

In December 2021, two months before the invasion of Ukraine and against the backdrop of the threat of more than 100,000 troops on Ukraine's eastern border, Vladimir Putin published two documents ("draft agreements") that, resembling unilateral, revisionist declarations, were intended to legitimise his breaches of international agreements after the fact. Moscow demanded full freedom of action in the post-Soviet space, called for a halt to NATO's eastward expansion and opposed the establishment of US military bases in non-NATO countries that were formerly part of the Soviet Union.[2]

As a counterreaction to Russia's destruction of the cooperative post-Cold War security order, the map of alliances and security cooperation has been redrawn. Finland has joined NATO, and, after the lifting of the Turkish veto, Sweden will too. Denmark has given up its opt-out from European security and defence cooperation. European countries are

---

2   Russia wanted to dissuade the US from any military cooperation with these countries in order to expand its own influence over them and, at the same time, to weaken the US militarily. During the military campaign in Afghanistan, for example, bases in the ex-Soviet republics of Uzbekistan and Kyrgyzstan played a central role for the US and its allies.

considering how to do more for their own security by stepping up spending and by improving cooperation to collectively make a bigger contribution to security on the European continent. This development builds on the frameworks for deeper defence cooperation set up at the EU level since 2017, including Permanent Structured Cooperation (PESCO) and the European Defence Fund. Back then, however, the strongest driver of European collaboration was not Russia's increasingly aggressive posture but the questions surrounding the reliability of the US commitment to NATO under the Trump administration.

Reasserting transatlantic ties

With Putin's attack on Ukraine, the importance of transatlantic ties has been underscored as vital, and the coordination on military supplies for Ukraine and sanctions has intensified. European countries' arms purchases from the US have increased, while energy diversification through the purchase of US liquefied natural gas (LNG) has contributed to rebalancing the external trade balance of the US vis-à-vis Europe. While no NATO member would downplay the existential nature of transatlantic security guarantees and the utmost importance of concrete US support to Ukraine, there is an acute awareness that the US is seeing the growing tensions with China as the much more consequential security challenge. Europe may hence need to step up spending on security in its eastern neighbourhood, while extending stronger support to US policies in Asia when a new US administration takes office in 2025.

Reviving EU enlargement

Within a year of the beginning of the war, not only has the debate on expanding NATO and strengthening European defence shifted, but the thinking around institutionalising ties with Eastern European and Southeast European countries has changed too. EU enlargement is back on the agenda: the political commitment to proceed more decidedly with the accession of the Western Balkan countries, the attempts to bring together the Open Balkan regional initiative and the Berlin Process, and, most of all, the granting of candidate status to Ukraine and the Republic of Moldova show that EU enlargement has been revived as a tool for bringing stability to the EU's eastern and southeastern neighbourhood.

To enhance stability on the European continent beyond the EU, new initiatives have been put forward to rethink and redesign security in its broadest sense on a continental scale. Russia's undermining of Europe's security order, the consequences for energy security, and the risk of a further rise of Russian and Chinese influence in increasingly fragile democracies on the border of the EU are driving a growing awareness that more needs to be done below full EU membership to work with EU neighbours. France's President Emmanuel Macron has suggested the creation of a European Political Community (EPC). Greeted with resistance by some countries at first, it has so far met twice and is the most tangible result of the ongoing rethink of a pan-European architecture of integration and partnerships. The EPC works as an intergovernmental format, whose value is to bring together over 40 heads of state and government for discussions about continental challenges, so far mostly in the fields of energy and security, while offering the opportunity for small group and bilateral meetings for conflict resolution.

The EPC has not been designed as an alternative to enlargement and includes countries that are unlikely to ever move into the EU. Full accession formally remains the goal for the countries that are negotiating or have received candidate status. But the triple challenge of driving accession negotiations, designing stronger preenlargement policies that effectively stabilise candidate countries in a much more hostile geopolitical environment, and reforming the EU internally should not be underestimated. Enlargement can take very long or can fail, which is why initiatives that allow stabilisation and a pushback on hostile influence are gaining importance. Meanwhile, a strong push for differentiation and a more loosely integrated group of countries may change the very nature of the EU as we know it.

Sanctions and building Europe's energy resilience

The reduction of Russian fossil energy imports because of sanctions and the diversification of energy relationships to other world regions, including the Gulf states and the US, has dramatically shrunk dependencies on Russia. By now, 11 sanction packages have been added to the previous ones imposed on Russia since 2014 in response to its annexation of Crimea and its failure to implement the Minsk agreements. Belarus has also been sanctioned for its support of the invasion, as has Iran for supplying drones to Russia. The packages combine economic and financial sanctions, sanctions on individuals, and visa measures.

In the area of energy, EU countries have forged new ties, or deepened existing ones, with other relevant providers, such as the US, Norway and the Gulf states. Internally, the investment into renewable energy, and measures to improve energy security within the single market and the Energy Union, which extends beyond the EU, are the first important steps towards more energy independence for the EU. High energy prices have driven the agreement between EU member states to start joint gas purchases and moved the European Commission into a central position in European energy policy.

The EU's overall sanction and energy-decoupling response, as well as arms deliveries to Ukraine, is shaped in close coordination with NATO, but also with other supporters of Ukraine outside Europe, such as Japan and Australia. The political West appears united, and cooperation across the Atlantic and within the G7 has been efficient and powerful. The West's political intention is to deprive Russia of the opportunity to continue the war. It has since become clear that, because of the significant decline in the supply of goods, Russia's economy is taking hits and the population's standard of living is deteriorating.[3] But the West has had to realise that its capacity to weaken Russia has limits: Russia has successfully established ways to circumvent the effect of sanctions, with, for instance, China being an increasingly important energy export destination and provider of goods, including dual-use products such as drones and trucks. Thus, the decisions that affect Russia's ability to pursue its expansionist policies are also being made outside the West – and decisions crucial to the conduct of the war and its end will in fact be taken in Beijing. China is increasingly seeking to position itself as a global player and mediator, and the relationship of EU member states with Russia will crucially depend on how Beijing lends its power and support to the country, its closest and yet much-weaker ally.

Economic shocks

The backdrop against which the political West and other key international players such as China design their policy responses to Russia's full-scale invasion of Ukraine is that of a severe economic downturn and a high-inflation environment. The war has indeed caused a massive shock to the global economy, squeezing supply and pushing up prices

---

3   For example, Russian revenues from oil and gas exports were down 20% from the previous year in autumn 2022. The automotive industry, which has directly or indirectly created 3.5 million jobs in Russia, had slumped by two thirds in autumn 2022 in comparison with 2021.

to unprecedented levels. Compared with other economic regions, the euro area and the EU economy have been particularly struck, given their economic openness, which makes them vulnerable to global market developments and value chain disruptions. This shock hit the European economy hard at a time of post-Covid recovery.

High inflation in the EU in 2022 resulted from the EU's high dependence on energy imports, which accounted for more than half of the euro area's energy use in 2020. Russia and Ukraine were also strong food and fertiliser providers before the start of the war. As a result, inflationary pressures, which were already comparatively high in the post-Covid-recovery phase, pushed up consumer prices, especially for energy and food, which accounted for more than two thirds of this record-high inflation in 2022. In 2023, food prices have become the most serious driver of inflation, after energy inflation in 2022. The two are intertwined: as food production is energy-intensive, food inflation is caused by lagged effects of high energy prices.

Risk factors: the geopolitics–economics nexus

Both geopolitical and economic factors put the future development of the EU at risk as it seeks to tackle its own twin climate and digital transitions. The repercussions for the democratic resilience of both transitions are potentially severe.

Stubborn inflation

The high dependence on energy imports has led to a large and unavoidable loss of real income, owing to the deterioration in Europe's terms of trade. Firms are needing to minimise their share of the burden by adjusting their pricing to fully recoup the increases in their input costs. Furthermore, workers are seeking to minimise their share of the burden by stepping up wage claims in a high-inflation environment in order to recoup real wage losses. While the European Central Bank is committed to pushing inflation back below 2%, there is a risk of a mutually reinforcing feedback loop between higher profit margins, nominal wages and prices. The social impact of high inflation makes this development far more than a monetary problem: low-income households in which food and energy constitute a large share of consumption are impacted in a particularly negative way. Consumer food inflation was in fact the largest component in euro area inflation. But as the war has moved into its second year, the European economy has demonstrated economic resilience to the effects of the war. Estimates point towards weak growth in the near term, as energy costs are coming down from peak levels in 2022 and fiscal measures are mitigating the impact of high inflation on real incomes. The unemployment rate even fell to its lowest level since the start of the euro area in 1999, reaching 6.6% in December 2022 and a record low of 6.4% in June 2023.

While food inflation has moderated, the war continues to pose significant risks to the economy. It is possible that the price of energy and food could rise again, with all the negative political and social consequences it would bring. Moreover, a lack of qualified labour may become a weakness in some sectors, provoking a relocation of certain activities away from Europe.

Competing industrial policies across the Atlantic

With the rising economic pressure, and the resulting political pressure, foreign and economic policy within the EU and in key partner countries has become more focused on its domestic and short-term effects. In the case of the US, the most striking example is the Inflation Reduction Act (IRA), a law of 16 August 2022 that marks the most significant action on clean energy and climate change in US history. The law is supposed to confront the existential threat of the climate crisis and set forth a new era of American innovation to lower consumer costs and drive global clean-energy economies. While the IRA constitutes an important move by the US in the fight against climate change, it is likewise a bold industrial policy programme. It will encourage investment inflows and job creation in the US, which are likely to weaken Europe. The negotiations with Europeans started only after the law was passed, and the IRA puts considerable pressure on Europeans to step up their own strategic industrial policy. This stance is not limited to the current Biden administration; the government that succeeds it will also be more focused on the domestic effects of economic and trade policy.

The geopolitical relevance of a transatlantic market space remains high, but policy on the US side will be driven by measures that promise short-term gains in terms of jobs, growth, investment inflows and competitive innovation. The fact that a more deeply integrated market would contribute to European derisking from China will only matter as a secondary factor. Longer-term orientations will only be pursued if the short-term decisions that lead to them come at low costs. It will be more difficult to point out win-win scenarios as the risk looms larger over Europe that the US will not necessarily consider closer trade, investment and tech-development ties as part of the US derisking strategy.

Fiscal pressure stress testing cohesion and democracy in Europe

In 2023, growth rates in the EU remain low, while debt and deficit levels in some EU countries have reached high levels and – if not corrected – may become unsustainable in the next few years. This would have several consequences. Governments will face tough trade-off decisions: on the one hand, they need to spend more on defence and other security-related policies, but, on the other, they may also face increasing pressures to cushion the effects of raised price levels for consumers and to bolster economic competitiveness and innovation capacities by more active industrial policies. The demand for a more proactive social policy as well as stronger industrial subsidies is high, as the US and China are resorting to very active state intervention in their respective national economies.

The price of energy will be one key factor: efforts to save energy and diversify supplies have contributed to a fall in natural gas prices after the record highs of autumn 2022. But the price of energy for the corporate sector is still seen as a major competitive disadvantage. Any national effort to compensate it will weigh on public finances and may distort competition within the single market. Moreover, there will likely be more national measures in addition to the REPowerEU initiative to help accelerate the transition to green energy and increase the EU's energy independence.

There are two risks inherent in increased domestic spending to foster energy transition, and they apply equally to digitalisation. The first is that divergence in the European Union may increase, as those regions that are most competitive may be able to translate support measures into tangible advantages more efficiently than weaker regions. Secondly, if governments keep up high deficits and further increase debt levels, this will not only raise interest payments but may make public debt more vulnerable to volatile markets. It is also likely that tensions over the role and quality of public finances will grow in the EU. A group of Nordic and Baltic countries will likely continue to argue for a return to the Stability and Growth Pact without major reforms, while other countries will request an extension of the NextGenerationEU fund or the creation of similar tools that allow joint borrowing on the markets or large transfers to economically weaker regions.

Tensions may rise not only between but also within countries over the question of adequate public spending and the role of the EU as a provider of European public goods. Potential further polarization between EU and national interests as well as criticism of the EU is likely to make EU decision-making more difficult and decisions potentially less legitimate. The increasing difficulty for democratically elected governments to deliver in times of crisis and to master deep transitions in a way that is perceived as just and equitable within societies may increase the likelihood of anti-EU positions among governments. Growing social and political tensions and related fears will be exploited by actors with a keen interest in weakening democracies. Since the beginning of the war, Russian interference through disinformation and cyberattacks on EU member states has risen. China also intensely interferes in European democracies, at times with more sophisticated measures. The resilience of democracies and attempts to improve their legitimacy on both the input and the output sides of policy-making will be a key issue for national and European policymakers, with the EU having the challenge of positioning itself as part of the solution while national policymakers may have increasing incentives to identify it as part of the problem.

What way forward? Issues at play for Europe and the transatlantic partnership

Amid the current crisis, the EU is once again facing policy and institutional design questions at the same time. The policy dimension does not only concern the immediate crisis response vis-à-vis Russia; two layers of challenges add to this. Firstly, there are growing socioeconomic pressures and the need to rethink economic and industrial policy in an increasingly competitive and geoeconomic world. Secondly, EU internal policies will have to be reformed and the financial tools adjusted ahead of a possible enlargement of the European Union, which will have distributive effects among today's members and could undermine the EU's success in preparing for its future in an even more challenging geopolitical and geoeconomic environment.

EU enlargement and reform: finding or losing the balance?

The two largest member states, Germany and France, have conditioned the further enlargement of the EU on internal reform but have not yet been able to build a consensus among themselves – let alone the other governments – on the exact goal of internal reforms and how they should be achieved. With Ukraine and Moldova having reached candidate status, and with a renewed commitment to bringing the Western Balkan countries into the EU, the costs of further enlargement to the current EU member states become obvious. Two examples illustrate this. Firstly, integrating Ukraine into the single market would bring in a large producer of agricultural goods, putting pressure on countries such as Poland and France. Secondly, bringing up to seven comparatively poor countries into the EU would make the current goals and funding of cohesion policy unsustainable. So there are substantial policy questions to solve that touch on key dimensions of the European Union's idea of itself and its internal solidarity, including what level of ambition for cohesion and convergence should be pursued with which funding tools. Current net recipients of EU funding such as Poland, although initially strongly supportive of Ukraine's accession, may turn into veto players. Meanwhile, the major net contributors to the EU budget are likely to have opposing views on the future funding of EU expenses (an issue that already divides France and Germany) and are likely to pressure for more rule-of-law conditionality in EU funding, since transferring money to countries in breach of European rule-of-law and democracy principles is seen as increasingly illegitimate. In addition to the challenge of adjusting EU funding, and in particular the next multiannual financial framework, to prepare for further EU enlargement, there is a major risk that no significant progress will be made on improving the EU's functioning.

Despite their jointly declared support for enlarging and deepening the EU, Germany and France's capacity to lead change in the European Union is reduced. Opposing views between member states on key policy and institutional challenges are one reason; difficult domestic circumstances in both of these major EU countries are another. In France, social unrest and a loss of support among the domestic public have reduced Macron's ability to lead, a possible victory for a far-right candidate in the next presidential election looms large, and far-right, anti-European perspectives have already gained more salience due to their strong presence in parliament. In Germany, a deeply divided three-party coalition and a finance ministry with very restrictive views on European and national public finances makes it unlikely that the government will take a strong leadership role in the EU.

Given the many variables at play across the EU, and uncertainty on the EU's reform agenda, three scenarios should be considered when exploring the future of the Union. The first and most ambitious is that the EU succeeds in implementing reforms internally (policies and budget, decision-making and institutions) and takes in up to eight new member states, while maintaining the current level of integration or even deepening it. It would overcome internal divisions over rule-of-law and democracy standards and secure respect for these principles, including in accession countries, such that net contributors continue to consider their transfers to other countries legitimate. The second scenario is that the EU does not substantially adjust its internal decision-making or its policies and their funding but takes in up to five Western Balkan countries, and possibly also Ukraine and Moldova if the conflict with Russia is settled in a way that guarantees stability for both countries. In this scenario, the EU enlarges but, as a group of up to 35, also loses decision-making capacity. It will not be able to sustain its goals for cohesion within the EU and divergence is likely to increase. This may then lead to a stronger push for a more differentiated EU, with a more deeply integrated core, likely led by Germany and France despite current disputes over energy, armament, fiscal rules and other issues. A third scenario is the creeping repatriation of competencies, and thus a less integrated EU. This can happen through the nonimplementation of European rules, even with commitments to the contrary. It can also entail deliberate disintegration decisions (meaning countries opting out of policies) or debates about further exits from the EU.

US policy after the elections: Atlantic bond or European divisions?

The role of the external drivers of internal disputes should not be underestimated. For example, striving for a deeper transatlantic relationship is a potentially divisive issue: some governments argue strongly for more European capacity to act independently of the US, pursuing France's long-standing aspiration to advance Europe's "strategic autonomy"; others, in particular those governments with a strong or full reliance on US military procurement, seek to avoid any suggestion that the EU is "turning away" from the US.

Europeans in any case need to prepare for a scenario in which the US no longer invests as much into European security as is currently the case. Not doing so would pose growing risks for the long-term viability of the transatlantic partnership. However, the main challenge for the transatlantic partnership may not come from Europe. A major risk for Europeans is an election victory of Donald Trump in 2024. Europeans would have to prepare for another four years or more of a nationalistic and unreliable US president who would probably once again seek to destroy structures of international order and the recently strengthened transatlantic relationship. Protectionist economic, financial and trade policies would be likely. Judging by the current radical rhetoric of the Republican Party on the power struggle with China, there could be an escalation of the relationship between Washington and Beijing.

The approach of different EU member states towards a US led once again by Donald Trump or a person with similar positions could divide the European Union. Points of contention would include not only security concerns but also attitudes towards political systems, in particular liberal democracy versus authoritarianism. Led by Donald Trump, the United States might again become a threat to democracy and cohesion in the European Union. In the case of the reelection of a Law and Justice (PiS) government in Poland, there could be an alliance across the Atlantic between two leaders keen to weaken the objective of a deeper and more integrated EU.

A not very likely but very consequential scenario should also be pondered: Trump singles out a PiS-led Poland as the US's main partner and access point to the EU – as Trump had selected British Prime Minister Boris Johnson and encouraged Brexit politically during his first term, while close friends of the then US president manipulated the Brexit campaign.[4] While the US reduces or drops its support for Ukraine, it promises a stronger engagement with Polish security, and encourages the reelected PiS leadership to pursue an authoritarian and nationalistic path in the EU, eventually encouraging Poland to partially disconnect from the EU, while other countries that no longer trust US security guarantees build a more deeply integrated core.

Finally, a wild card is Trump's liking for authoritarian leaders. This suggests a less likely but extremely damaging scenario in which Trump forges some kind of authoritarian alliance, leaving the camp of the political West by both destroying US democracy as we know it and pulling the US out of Western-built multilateralist structures and bilateral relationships. Even worse, this scenario would still include the possibility of a major conflict between the US and China, as the relationship between authoritarian leaders may be prone to disruptions and self-interested behaviour.

---

4 Cadwalladr, C. (2017) "The great British Brexit robbery: how our democracy was hijacked". *The Guardian*, 7 May.

Recommendations for the EU

Today, most political attention is focused on the transatlantic allies' support for Ukraine in terms of military provisions and financial and humanitarian aid, on managing the twin climate and digital transitions, and on making European states and societies more resilient to external challenges. But the most strategically important question for the EU member states and the US that needs tackling now is whether and how, after a possible end to the war, a new rules-based and cooperative security order can be built on the European continent, or whether Europeans must build a security order without or against Russia in the long term.

Under any scenario, the EU will need to engage more in terms of security in its east and its eastern neighbourhood, which means its members need to spend more and cooperate more effectively. Regarding enlargement policy, the EU should avoid a scenario in which accession fails and European influence in its neighbourhood declines. With a view to that, the EU should set a target date for when it will be ready to welcome new members and focus efforts on preparing the EU internally, while clearly signalling to the candidate countries what is expected from them and which offers can be made in the short term as part of an effort to support and stabilise them. At the same time, the EU should use other available tools such as the EPC, deeper trade relations and the Energy Union to enhance security and stability as well as democratic transition in partner countries across the continent. The overall goal should be enhancing stability and security on a continental scale, even if the necessary adaptations in the EU to accommodate up to eight new members, and the necessary transformations in the candidate countries, take longer than expected or cannot be achieved, which would challenge the prospect of full accession. If Europe does not play a stronger role in Europe's east and, simultaneously, does not engage more strongly with Washington to uphold security in Asia, then US engagement on the European continent will very likely decline. This would decisively amplify the stabilisation task of the EU. The outcome of the US elections in 2024 will crucially impact the outlook for Europe, and the EU would-be well advised to invest heavily into diplomacy now (in security, defence, industrial policy, tech) in order to tighten the relationship with the US in a way that is of mutual interest.

Within the EU, strategies to regain competitiveness, ensure societal cohesion and strengthen the resilience of democracies are key. Because of multiple crises and their economic effects, the internal socioeconomic outlook is fragile. But a certain degree of socioeconomic cohesion within and between societies is key to managing the twin transitions and sustaining democracies. And European governments need to make sure that budgetary tools are designed and implemented in the best possible way in view of these challenges. This means, firstly, that the currently available funding from NextGenerationEU is deployed effectively and quickly. In parallel, the EU needs to improve financing opportunities in the single market through the completion of the capital markets union and through forward-looking budgetary policies at the EU and national levels that support private investment in the big transition tasks the EU is facing. Public investment needs to support Europe's current catch-up process vis-à-vis China and the US. The upcoming European Parliament elections and different national and regional elections in 2024 will be a litmus test for whether the EU is successfully managing yet another substantial crisis while improving its own functioning and global role at the same time.

Giovanni Grevi

Conclusion: averting a regressive world – global trends and Europe's leadership

Short spans of time can crystallise developments that have long been building, and they can spur far-reaching change. The year 2022 has been one of those times. In February, Russia launched the full-scale invasion of Ukraine shortly after the publication of a joint Sino-Russian revisionist manifesto calling for a new world order. During the same weeks, statistics reported that in 2021 China's economy had overtaken that of the European Union in size. In March the Intergovernmental Panel on Climate Change released a report warning that the window of opportunity to prevent catastrophic climate change is closing. By spring 2022 the war had sparked energy and food price inflation, engendering a worldwide cost-of-living crisis. Over the course of the year, alongside the brutal invasion of Ukraine and growing tensions between the US and China, trade between China and Russia climbed 50%, while trade between China and both the US and the EU broke new records. Towards the end of 2022, the global population crossed the 8 billion threshold, with more than one in four suffering from food insecurity, about 200 million facing sheer hunger and 108 million forcibly displaced.

In a nutshell, these few pointers convey the story of a world that is splintered by (geo)politics yet bound by all sorts of flows and de facto united in facing profound transnational challenges. Given this background, what is the long-term impact of Russia's war in Ukraine on an increasingly turbulent and interconnected world?

The seven thematic chapters collected in this book offer an in-depth assessment of the repercussions of Russia's attack on Ukraine for different dimensions of international affairs, with a horizon of around 2030. In doing so they highlight drivers and directions of change, challenges ahead and policy implications that are specific to each of these domains.

However, various common patterns clearly emerge from several contributions. These are some of the systemic trends that are expected to shape developments across various policy areas and the international order at large.

The merit of foresight consists precisely in stepping back from distinct factors of change to explore their interconnections, and from the emergencies of the day – as compelling as they are – to assess the broad direction and potential outcomes of change.[1] Assessing the evolution of current trends also requires considering the events that might accelerate them, alter their course or even reverse them. At the same time, the impact of these events will very much depend on the context in which they take place. Sparks trigger large wildfires in dry and untended woods, much less so in healthy, well-managed forests.

This chapter sketches out some cross-cutting perspectives on what the future might hold for the international order following Russia's attack against Ukraine in 2022, and it calls for European leadership to help steer the world away from systemic regression. The first section reviews three broad directions of change shaping the international order. The second section outlines three main "switch" factors, each of them harbouring systemic consequences with the potential to steer the international order in very different directions and create diverse sets of challenges and opportunities for the EU. The third section outlines the scenario of a regressive world – one where the relatively progressive trends that unfolded since the end of the Cold War are definitively reversed and the world drifts towards a new normal of instability, power politics, economic fracturing and deepening global challenges. The fourth section turns to the EU, exploring some of the difficult choices, trade-offs and dilemmas facing the Union over the next institutional cycle and beyond. The fifth and concluding section argues that the EU needs to decisively shift from firefighting (short term and piecemeal approaches to crises and challenges) to forest management, deploying structural reforms and policies to strengthen its resilience and global leadership.

---

1 For an early assessment of the consequences of Russia's aggression of Ukraine from a European standpoint, see Grevi, G. (2023) "Terra incognita: exploring the long-term implications of the war in Ukraine". FEPS Policy Brief, February.

Directions of change

Between "slowbalisation" and splintering globalisation

All the contributions to this book stress that globalisation is at high risk of splintering, and multilateralism of cracking, under the weight of great power rivalry. Geopolitics is affecting all levels of interdependence, amplifying the mutual vulnerabilities of highly connected actors and reducing scope for cooperation. From this standpoint, the war in Ukraine has been less a turning point than a powerful boost to a trend already well underway.

The geopolitical contagion is spreading through the multilateral system, carried by various vectors such as resurgent nationalism, polarising narratives, aggressive behaviour and the weaponisation of interdependence. The systemic rivalry between the US and China is the principal, structural manifestation of this major trend. It is also a rivalry that risks setting the tone for international politics and economics at large, normalising an antagonistic attitude that may turn into a self-fulfilling prophecy. At the same time, both Washington and Beijing are aware that the weaponisation of interdependence carries not only large, foreseeable economic costs but also major unpredictable risks, whether in terms of unintended escalation or failure to manage shared challenges.

In this volatile context Russia's aggression has both multiplied risks and determined new fractures. This has certainly been the case for energy markets.[2] In addition to the most obvious discontinuity – the collapse of the energy partnership between Russia and Europe – the war has triggered the redirection of international energy flows, determined a steep spike in prices and enhanced the competitive position of major Gulf exporters while damaging Russia's long-term status as an energy superpower. In short, the war has accentuated the prevalence of geopolitical considerations over economic ones in the shaping of increasingly fragmented fossil fuels markets.

The perfect energy security storm caused by Russia's aggression has heavily impacted the developing world too, given heightened competition for gas supplies and price inflation for energy and food commodities. The war in Ukraine has aggravated the development challenges that the pandemic had already exacerbated, leading to serious setbacks on the road to achieving Agenda 2030. In an unfavourable economic context

---

2 See Chapter 2, by Thijs Van de Graaf, and Chapter 3, by Thomas Pellerin-Carlin.

marked by modest growth prospects for the main donors, high interest rates and growing risk of debt distress, the coming years are likely to witness a mismatch between the financing needs of developing countries and constrained development finance.[3] Geopolitical tensions between China and traditional donors might further complicate progress on the development agenda – yet another instance of power politics undermining global public goods.

Several contributions to this book have also pointed to the incremental redirection of trade and investment flows, which are increasingly reflecting emerging geopolitical alignments.[4] Despite some differences in the transatlantic debate on China, both the US and the EU have taken, or are considering, several measures to derisk economic relations with Beijing. Derisking or decoupling, however, are not Western prerogatives. China is seeking to lower its vulnerability to the world while enhancing the dependence of others on China's exports in critical domains, such as green technologies. Global foreign direct investment flows have already fallen from an average of 3.3% of global gross domestic product (GDP) in the 2000s to around 1.3% over the 2018–2022 period, and a growing literature points to the long-term costs of the fragmentation of economic flows.[5] At the same time, despite successive disruptions and rising geopolitical tensions, economic globalisation has so far proved quite resilient. Recent findings show that economic flows have strongly rebounded, and continue to expand, after plunging due to the Covid pandemic in 2020, while evidence of a sustained regionalisation of flows is limited.[6] The weight of America and China as a share of respective overall global flows has decreased since 2016, but this trend has not led to a wider decoupling of the global economy.[7] Yet the fact that it has not does not mean that it will not: various factors point to fragmentation, but the extent of it remains uncertain.

The war in Ukraine may weaken the global economic order in other ways too, through the long-term effect of the unprecedented Western economic sanctions inflicted on Russia.[8] Alongside military support to

---

3 See Chapter 6, by Annalisa Prizzon.
4 See Chapter 4, by George Papaconstantinou, and Chapter 5, by Elvire Fabry.
5 International Monetary Fund (2023) "World economic outlook: a rocky recovery". Report, IMF, April.
6 Altman, S. A., and Bastian, C. R. (2023) "DHL Global Connectedness Index 2022". DHL in partnership with NYU Stern, February.
7 Ibid.
8 See Chapter 4, by Papaconstantinou.

Ukraine, sanctions are an essential component of the strategy to counter Russia's war of aggression and limit its capacity to launch future attacks. They have undoubtedly depressed Russia's growth prospects and shrunk the scope for diversifying its economy away from commodity exports, but so far they have not crippled Russia's war effort. Looking ahead, the broader question is whether the West leveraging its predominant position in the financial sector will induce others to seek alternatives to the role of the US dollar and the euro as reserve and payment currencies, developing financial circuits insulated from Western pressure. Such developments would be highly disruptive of globalisation, and damaging for the influence and network power of the US in particular. Despite vocal statements and some modest steps in this direction, such as those by the BRICS countries, [9] the conditions for a break with the current financial and monetary systems appear far from materialising. China faces a profound unresolved dilemma between asserting state control over the economy (the current priority) and enabling the internationalisation of the renminbi, which requires deep and liquid capital markets and credible rule of law. However, the sanctions deployed by the West in response to Russia's aggression have focused minds in parts of the non-Western world on how to reduce vulnerabilities to the weaponisation of finance.

Multipolar bricolage

Russia's war in Ukraine has further polarised global politics but has not delineated a definitive path towards a new international order.[10] Depending on the (shifting) distribution of different power resources, and on how they will be converted into actual influence, the shape of the international order in the making could look quite different. The US maintains an edge (if in many ways an eroding one) over its rivals in multiple domains, from the military to key sectors of technological innovation and international finance, not to mention the vast range of US allies and partners. When considering the weight of rising powers in the trade, energy or development orders, the world is increasingly multipolar, even though the US, China and the EU stand out as economic powers in their own league. Despite growing economic challenges, China might still match or overtake the

---

9 Brazil, Russia, India, China and South Africa.

10 For an assessment of the impact of the war in Ukraine on multipolar competition, see Biscop, S. (2023) "War for Ukraine and the rediscovery of geopolitics: must the EU draw new battlelines or keep an open door?" Egmont Paper 123, June (https://www.egmontinstitute.be/war-for-ukraine-and-the-rediscovery-of-geopolitics/).

US in terms of aggregate power by the middle of the century. However, many factors might either anticipate or indefinitely delay this tipping point. Besides, the issue remains how China will or will not be able to wield its power to acquire influence and shape an international order in line with its preferences. Through so-called discursive power (the capacity to generate and spread narratives and world views), a growing range of actors – from China and Russia to the Gulf countries or Brazil – are willing and increasingly able to challenge, or at least offer alternatives to, Western world views.

The fact that much of "the rest" has not followed the West in taking determined action to stop Russia reflects, therefore, deeper shifts in international relations.[11] The trend towards the emergence of a much more heterogeneous, diverse and contested world in terms of narratives and values has long been detected.[12] The issue is not so much that positions are growing more divergent on the global stage but that those holding divergent views are acquiring more voice with which to assert them. The variety of perspectives surrounding the war in Ukraine is a manifestation of this underlying pattern of change – although a particularly visible one, given the salience of the issues at stake.

Beyond assessing the distribution of power assets and the competition of world views, the larger point is that the costs of using power, in particular for coercive purposes, are growing. Russia's attack against Ukraine provides multiple lessons from this standpoint. Far superior to Kyiv on paper, Moscow has failed to prevail in the field and has degraded its own power base, but it might still be able to prevent others – Ukraine and its Western partners – from achieving their goals. Meanwhile, the US and European allies have provided massive support to Ukraine, but within the limits of their own confined resources, of other strategic priorities (such as in the Indo-Pacific for the US) and of concerns about avoiding escalation. China, on the other side, appears to be doing enough to avoid Russia's economic collapse, while avoiding confronting the West over Ukraine. This might foreshadow a world of powers that are as constrained as they are mighty.

---

11   Over the course of 2022, Michel Duclos at the Institut Montaigne has directed a series of contributions – "Ukraine shifting the world order" – delivering a variety of perspectives on the roots and implications of the war in Ukraine from various countries and regions.

12   See, for example, Grevi, G., Keohane, D., Lee, B., and Lewis, P. (2013) "Empowering Europe's future: governance, power and options for the EU in a changing world". European Strategy and Policy Analysis System (ESPAS), European Union, December.

While it is hard to anticipate the destination of the ongoing power transition, for the foreseeable future the international order will likely feature some form of bifurcated multipolarity.[13] In other words, it will become an order where various powers hold sufficient confidence and resources to pursue their own interests with a degree of autonomy, but where the rivalry between the US and China exerts a growing pull factor on most of them. The strength of this factor will depend on the form and intensity of the Sino-American rivalry. The many strategic, ideological and military variables that will shape it cannot be reviewed here. A potential clash around Taiwan is widely identified as the spark that could ignite a conflict between the superpowers. Among the economic factors that will shape competition between Washington and Beijing, respective growth rates, technological achievements and leadership of broader geoeconomic coalitions have been highlighted in this book.[14]

In a fluid and contested strategic context, blanket notions such as the so-called Global South or "the West and the rest" are unhelpful to describe the state of play and to capture developments ahead. Boxing into one category those countries that have not taken a firm position on Russia's aggression blurs their important differences. Some countries may fit the definition of "swing states" – amenable to switching sides within parameters broadly defined by others. What the war in Ukraine has exposed, however, is that an increasing number of countries aspire to advance their own agendas, independently of the efforts of others to sway them in different directions. To be sure, this is not necessarily a trend that will bolster international law and multilateralism, as the agnosticism of parts of the international community concerning Russia's aggression proves.

The consolidation of a largely bipolar order framed by Sino-American competition cannot be ruled out in the long term. However, the next decade is more likely to see the spread of multipolar bricolage, with powers large and small testing the waters, and their means of influence, while keeping a rather pragmatic and flexible approach so as to diversify their geopolitical portfolio. The applications of an otherwise very diverse range of countries to join the BRICS forum, and the recent expansion of the latter to include six new members, foreshadows this development. The same goes for the attempt of middle powers such as Turkey or Saudi Arabia to present themselves as mediators between Russia and Ukraine, while gaining status on the international stage.

---

13   Higgott, R., and Reich, S. (2022) "It's bifurcation, not bipolarity: understanding world order after the Ukraine invasion". CSDS Policy Brief 16, July.

14   See Chapter 4, by Papaconstantinou, and Chapter 5, by Fabry.

The emergence of multipolar regions worldwide is another trend expected to intensify, with great powers extending their reach through a mix of narratives, dialogues, incentives and coercion, and local powers hedging their bets through multivector foreign policies. The growing presence of China and Russia across the Middle East and Africa is of course a consequential development for Europe and, at least in the case of China, one likely to persist well into the future.

An unsustainable world

The long-term implications of Russia's aggression of Ukraine will not be limited to geopolitics and economics. They might also enduringly affect the capacity of the international community to deliver global public goods, such as global health and a clean environment. Russia's war risks aggravating the deficit of responsibility and trust that already hindered cooperation to deal with pressing transnational challenges.[15] Among them, the consequences of climate change are no longer just a subject of projections into the distant future. They are a matter of clear and present danger.

The year 2023 is well on track to beat some of the negative records established in 2022. July 2023 went down as the hottest ever registered, and this is part of a pattern, not an exception. To put this in perspective, temperatures in July are estimated to have reached 1.5 °C above the pre-industrial average.[16] This is the threshold set at COP21 in Paris (the 2015 United Nations Climate Change Conference), above which the chances of climate change carrying disastrous effects rise dramatically. According to the World Meteorological Organization, the likelihood of average global temperatures exceeding preindustrial levels by more than 1.5 °C for at least a year between 2023 and 2028 stands at 66%.[17] In short, scientific findings point to the fact that global warming is proceeding faster than expected.

---

15 For stark warnings of the dangers facing the international community, and proposals on how to strengthen international cooperation, see United Nations (2021) "Our common agenda", report of the Secretary General, September; and Olof Palme International Center, International Peace Bureau and International Trade Union Confederation (2022) "Common security 2022: for our shared future", April.

16 Copernicus Climate Change Service (2023) "July 2023: global earth and ocean temperatures reach new record highs". Press release, 8 August.

17 World Meteorological Organization (2023) "Global annual to decadal climate update". Report, WMO, May.

It is understood that climate change amplifies a range of connected risks and threats – for example, by harming food production (and therefore security), heightening health threats and multiplying drivers of conflict.[18] The fact that an estimated 90% of refugees come from the countries most vulnerable to climate change offers a clear glimpse into future human (in)security. Climate change also poses a growing threat to energy security, via, for example, potential damage to energy infrastructure along coastlines.[19] Considering the cumulative effect of climate change and other transnational challenges such as pandemics, the UN Secretary General concluded that "humankind is making the world an increasingly insecure and precarious place", affecting human security worldwide.[20]

The roots of these trends are deep and their impact is exacerbated by vast socioeconomic inequalities within and between countries, hitting the most vulnerable the hardest. Mitigating these trends will depend on cooperatively shaping a fair balance of responsibility between developing and advanced countries, with the latter boosting their contributions at all levels. However, in a world already strained by the Covid pandemic and the deep 2020 recession, Russia's full-scale invasion of Ukraine has aggravated challenges to sustainable development and human security in both direct and indirect ways. The former include the traumatic supply shock that hit energy and food markets in 2022, resulting in a twin cost-of-living and debt crisis and affecting the livelihoods of hundreds of millions.[21] This is far from over. After withdrawing from the grain deal that allowed for the export of cereals through the Black Sea, within a few days Russia launched strikes that reportedly destroyed 180,000 tons of grain stored in Ukraine, and several port infrastructures, to further cripple the country's revenues, and attacks continued throughout summer.[22]

---

18   United Nations Development Programme (2022) "New threats to human security in the Anthropocene: demanding greater solidarity", special report, February; Stockholm International Peace Research Institute (2022) "Environment of peace: security in a new era of risk", report, May.
19   See Chapter 2, by Van de Graaf.
20   United Nations Development Programme (2022) "New threats to human security in the Anthropocene", foreword.
21   UN Global Crisis Response Group on Food, Energy and Finance (2022) "Global impact of the war in Ukraine: billions of people face the greatest cost-of-living crisis in a generation". Brief 2, United Nations, 8 June.
22   Polityuk, P. (2023) "Russia strikes Ukraine's Danube port, driving up global grain prices". *Reuters*, 3 August.

Russia's war is contributing to an unsustainable world in broader ways too, by diverting both financial and political capital away from cooperation and towards heightened competition. First, as noted above, the war has reduced the growth prospects and therefore the fiscal space of many Western donors, forcing difficult trade-offs between domestic spending priorities (such as energy subsidies, defence expenditure and support for Ukrainian refugees in Europe) and assisting developing countries.[23] Considering the response to humanitarian crises, in 2022 the UN estimated that about $49 billion would be required over the course of the year, but that available resources amounted to only a third of that – the biggest funding gap ever faced.[24]

Second, the war is draining trust and deepening cleavages between major powers. This might carry particularly detrimental long-term effects for cooperation on climate change, and for the viability of the energy transition. The latter depends on massively expanding investment into renewable energy and infrastructure, and on the resilience of the supply chains for the materials and green technologies required to match fast-expanding demand. Geopolitical tensions and geoeconomic competition, in particular between China and the West, threaten to disrupt these flows, to affect technological innovation and to lead to separate regulatory regimes.[25] That would in turn entail inflationary pressures and make the transition more expensive, which would slow it down and aggravate climate change.

Switch factors

The directions of change broadly outlined here are of course subject to considerable variations. The future is defined not just by large trends but also by their interplay with disruptive events and human agency. Having reviewed how the outbreak of the war in Ukraine has affected the pace and trajectory of some key trends, it is important to turn to the switch factors that might shape their evolution, and to the scenarios that they might lead to. Of the many variables that can be foreseen, including wild cards such as new virulent global pandemics, this section focuses on three

---

23 See Chapter 6, by Prizzon.
24 Fassihi, F. (2022)"U.N. faces record humanitarian aid shortfall – but not for Ukrainians". *New York Times*, 22 August.
25 Demarais, A. (2023) "How climate change will reshape economic statecraft", Carnegie Endowment for International Peace website, 20 June. See also Chapter 5, by Fabry, in this book.

that are pivotal to the future of the international order and to Europe's place therein.

The outcome of Russia's war in Ukraine

The first major switch factor is the course and outcome of the war in Ukraine itself. On this score, there are three main uncertainties. The first concerns whether the war will escalate– including through the potential use of nuclear weapons – and involve other parties, notably NATO. The second is about who will prevail, and over what timeframe, along the spectrum ranging from Ukrainian victory to Russian success. A third uncertainty is what sort of Russia Europe and the West will face when the fight ends.[26]

The extent to which the war will shape global power balances down the line, among many other variables, can be debated. But it is hard to deny that it will prove consequential under any scenario. Were the US and its allies to be directly dragged into the conflict, the war might usher in a paradigm shift with potentially devastating consequences (beyond the dramatic pain already inflicted on Ukraine), all the more so if this followed Russia taking recourse to nuclear weapons. This remains a very unlikely but nevertheless very high-impact scenario for the future of the international order and global security.

Even assuming that such a catastrophe will not occur, the outcome of the war will inevitably set a precedent in terms of the costs of military aggression, the gains that it can bring, the capacity of the international community to repel it and the currency of neoimperial revisionist worldviews – such as that expressed by Russia – in international affairs. Moscow's success would affect the perceptions of broader power trajectories, weakening the standing of the US and its allies in the face of surging competitors. Such perceptions may or may not correspond to actual patterns of rise and decline, measured by assets such as the economy, technology and military capabilities. But they might still shape the calculus of a wide range of actors that have taken a pragmatic approach to managing geopolitical uncertainty, and that may adjust their bets in response. There is also a risk that Russia's success would embolden China to seek a military solution to tensions around Taiwan. It is unclear what the impact of a potential Ukrainian defeat might be in Europe and across the Atlantic – whether it would buttress unity against the Russian

---

26 See Chapter 1, by Andriy Korniychuk.

threat, or precipitate mutual recriminations and divisions among allies. The quality of American leadership would likely be decisive at such a dramatic juncture.

More or less the reverse considerations would apply were Ukraine to prevail and Russia to pull back. The defeat of the aggressor by Kyiv and the large international coalition supporting its war effort would resonate widely. It would reassert basic principles of international law, undermine the appeal of authoritarian revisionist regimes, confirm the reliability of the US in the eyes of both partners and rivals, and deter adversaries. Russia's defeat might also open up new scenarios involving potential regime change in Moscow and, some argue, calling into question the resilience of the Russian state itself in the face of centrifugal forces. Prospects for some sort of liberal revolution in Russia in the short term appear very slim, although a traumatic defeat could either disrupt domestic politics or plant the seeds for change over time. Alternatives range from an even more radicalised Russian leadership seeking revenge down the line to a regime absorbed by damage limitation, but still hostile to the West.

In between these two scenarios lies that of a protracted, painful and inconclusive struggle. Given the political costs for either party to compromise, a grinding war could last for years, perhaps alternating between active and dormant phases, until the balance of incentives shifts and enables an acceptable ceasefire or peace deal. Under this scenario, Russia's power assets would continue to degrade across all dimensions, but Moscow would remain capable of threatening not only Ukraine but also Western interests worldwide. Whether a protracted war would per se exacerbate the rivalry between the US and China would depend on a wider range of factors. Chief among them would be the extent and nature of China's support to Russia. But it is likely that an open conflict would complicate efforts at improving the strategic dialogue between Washington and Beijing, and impair international cooperation at large. In other words, the scenario of a protracted war is not necessarily one of relative stability (beyond Ukraine) but one making the international order more vulnerable to disruption, eroding the platforms for dialogue and the boundaries of competition.

The 2024 US presidential elections

The result of the US presidential election in November 2024 is another pivotal switch factor and, potentially, a very uncomfortable one to contemplate for Europe. Russia's aggression of Ukraine has underscored the essential role of the transatlantic partnership and NATO for European defence. The EU and the US have fostered dialogues on a broad range of topics on the bilateral and global agendas under the Biden administration, including the implications of China's rise and assertiveness. Developments on the international stage suggest that transatlantic cooperation would be of increasing salience to meeting shared priorities, while also engaging other partners. Whether the transatlantic partnership will live up to its potential will depend, however, on variables both external and internal to Europe and the US. Developments in American domestic politics will be a decisive factor in the short-term. Donald Trump seems on course to win the Republican primaries, which would lead him to challenge President Biden next year. Seeking to guess at this stage who will be sworn in as the 47th president of the US is pointless. But it is significant that a recent poll showed that voting intentions for Biden and for Trump stood at the same level: 43%.[27] What is clear is that, for the rest of the world, these are the most consequential American elections in many decades – a potential game-changer.

This significance is due both to the volatile global context and to the unique features of Trump's leadership and agenda. The strategic environment is much more fluid and dangerous than the relatively more stable world of 2017, when Trump took office. On top of that, a second-time President Trump might shift US foreign policy priorities more drastically and rapidly than he was able or willing to do back then. This is not a foregone conclusion. Aspects of continuity and discontinuity coexisted throughout successive US administrations. An increasing focus on domestic priorities, efforts to reduce American commitments abroad (except for core national interests) and growing concentration on the Indo-Pacific have been defining features of American grand strategy under the Obama, Trump and Biden administrations, and they would likely frame the agenda of a second Biden term too. However, Trump's approach broke with any post-World War II US administration because of the delinking of American national interests from broader global responsibilities.[28] Trump regarded the international order not as a multiplier of US influence but a drain on US power and a brake on its freedom of action. In short, Trump asserted a nationalist and populist narrative framing US priorities. There

---

27   Epstein, J. R., Igielnik, R., and Baken, C. (2023) "Biden shores up Democratic support, but faces tight race against Trump". *New York Times*, 1 August.
28   Grevi, G. (2017) "Trump's America: the ordinary superpower". Discussion Paper, European Policy Centre, June.

is little reason to believe that a second Trump administration would take a different course.

On some aspects of the international agenda, there was indeed a gap between Trump's disruptive rhetoric and relative continuity in American foreign policy, as seen, for example, in the enduring US contribution to European defence via NATO. However, today the stakes are much higher, and Trump might well feel less bound by legacy policies. This also applies to the US commitment to support Ukraine against Russia – which Trump has been very ambivalent about, while boasting that he would end the war "within 24 hours"[29] – and to relations with China, which are addressed below.

The possible reelection of Trump in 2024 would likely deal a heavy blow to transatlantic relations and in particular to US–EU ties. The fundamental normative disconnect between Trump and the EU rests on the opposition between unilateralism and multilateralism, nationalism and supranationalism, "America first" and a genuine transatlantic partnership. This disconnect would fuel divergence on multiple dossiers, not least considering the controversies that already surround respective industrial and regulatory policies and their repercussions across the Atlantic. Trump may seek to nurture closer partnerships with those EU member states that are more ideologically aligned to him, or that are eager to obtain additional US security guarantees beyond those offered by a potentially weakened NATO.[30] By pursuing bilateral partnerships, a second Trump administration might therefore sharpen divisions among Europeans, which would in turn reduce the ability of the EU to define its own policies on contentious matters on the transatlantic agenda. From being a key factor of European convergence under President Biden when leading the response to Russia's war against Ukraine, the US under Trump might become a key factor of European and transatlantic fragmentation.

The trajectory of the US–China rivalry

When dealing with the future, nothing is cast in stone. But when seeking to assess prospects for Sino-American relations, it is difficult to miss the factors that point to more turbulence in an already strained relationship. Russia's war in Ukraine is not the principal driver of US–China rivalry, but it is a complicating factor. It is a polarising issue in respective narratives,

---

29   Slisco, A. (2023) "Trump says he could end Russia's war 'within 24 hours' of negotiation". *Newsweek*, 26 January.
30   See Chapter 7, by Daniela Schwarzer.

a major irritant in the daily exchanges between the US and China at the bilateral and multilateral levels, and a conflict that neither superpower wishes their partners to lose. It follows that, on top of challenging the very foundations of international law, Russia's war in Ukraine has become another, dramatic front of the wider hegemonic competition between the US and China.

Of course, a highly disruptive switch factor in this context of intense competition would be China's military aggression against Taiwan, triggering a response by the US and its allies. Various contributions to this book refer to this event as a potential systemic disruption that, leaving aside the risk of escalation into a full-fledged regional or global war, would collapse globalisation, economic growth and multilateralism.[31] Even if the conflict could be contained in scale and time, its consequences would be momentous in terms of defining the balance of power, of rules and of narratives in the future international order, all the more so if China were to prevail and seize the island. It is difficult to anticipate the likelihood of China attacking Taiwan but, among other factors, the military build-up around the Taiwan Strait, China's increasingly aggressive military posture and nationalistic rhetoric, and some oscillations in the American debate about US policy on cross-Strait relations[32] suggest that a conflict scenario cannot be ruled out.

Even if a conflict over Taiwan does not take place, the evolution and implications of the Sino-American rivalry will remain the most important variable structuring the international order. The factors that have driven the deterioration of the relationship between Washington and Beijing in the last few years are unlikely to evaporate in the foreseeable future. The question is whether they will be aggravated or managed. These factors include mutual strategic concerns, economic and technological competition, lack of trust, ideological opposition, and the surge of antagonistic narratives in respective public spheres. The common denominator to all dimension of Sino-American competition is the prospect of hegemonic power transition, which makes China and the US each other's defining priority. The US has openly identified China as the only systemic challenger to American primacy and to the liberal international order. China sees the

---

[31] See Chapter 1, by Korniychuk, Chapter 4, by Papaconstantinou, and Chapter 5, by Fabry.

[32] Task Force on US–China Policy (2022) "Avoiding war over Taiwan". Policy brief, Asia Society, Center on US–China Relations, and UC San Diego School of Global Public Policy and Strategy, 21st Century China Center.

US as intent on suppressing its rise as it strives to become the world's preeminent power.

The Sino-American rivalry has extended not only across a widening range of sectors in bilateral relations, notably the race for technological leadership, but also across most global regions and multilateral frameworks. There is a risk that systemic competition will lead over time to systemic decoupling by both sides. This would in turn result in the long-term splintering of globalisation and of the global order into two broad spheres of influence, rules and narratives – what has been termed "*bi-mondialisation*".[33] However, whether the hegemonic struggle between the US and China will lead to an ever-more-pronounced bifurcation of the international order, or to a new Cold War, will depend not just on their priorities but also on those of other pivotal actors. Strategic hedging can be expected to drive the approach of regional powers and groupings as they seek to preserve their autonomy and escape the creeping bipolarisation of international affairs.

As pointed out above, amid an increasingly adversarial relationship, there is an understanding in Washington and Beijing of the deep interdependence binding them, of their interest in preventing the global order from unravelling and of the destabilising potential of their rivalry. Recent high-level meetings between top representatives from the two governments reflect ongoing attempts at managing competition, as presidents Biden and Xi wished for in autumn 2022. However, efforts to do so are increasingly overshadowed by polarising narratives and antagonistic moves. China is very outspoken in contesting what it regards as the US- or Western-led international order and is deploying multiple initiatives to challenge it, including on the multilateral stage. Many have noted that ideology and security concerns increasingly appear to trump economic interests in defining China's priorities, even at a time when China's growth model has lost steam. At the same time, Beijing needs a relatively open and stable international order if it is to fulfil the paramount goal that its own rise and credibility ultimately depend on: revamping and sustaining economic growth.

In Washington the bipartisan consensus on out-competing China and preserving US primacy will likely endure beyond the upcoming presidential elections. However, the possible victory of Trump might entail significant variations in the US approach. Trump might well take a more muscular stance towards China, which would sharpen tensions and

---

33 Ekman, A. (2022) *Dernier vol pour Pékin* (Paris: Éditions de l'Observatoire).

further bipolarise the international order. A less likely, but not implausible, scenario would see Trump seeking some sort of deal among the two superpowers (as he attempted to do early in his first term), possibly by using maximum geoeconomic pressure to bring Beijing to the table. It is difficult to envisage China being coerced into compromise, but it is not to be excluded that some transaction could be achieved through a mix of mutual threats and offers. A Trump administration would be unlikely to make ideological or normative differences an obstacle to that. Such deals would probably marginalise both other players (including respective partners) and multilateral frameworks.

Business as usual: the spectre of a regressive world

The review provided here of some of the main global trends, and of selected switch factors that could shape their course, is not meant to be exhaustive. This exercise started with the question of how Russia's aggression of Ukraine might affect various aspects of international affairs over the long term, and what that means for the international order and for Europe. Consequential dimensions of change that are not primarily related to the ongoing war, such as future patterns of technological innovation and the massive opportunities and challenges that they harbour, have therefore not been addressed as such. While not comprehensive, this assessment underscores that exploring the implications of the war in Ukraine requires considering the structural shifts that preceded, surround and will follow the conflict. When doing so, the case can be made that Russia's aggression risks marking a tipping point, turning a volatile and contested world into one facing lasting regression.

This is not a factual finding, and even less a prediction, but something akin to a median course between a best-case scenario of renewed rules-based cooperation and political convergence, on the one end, and a worst-case scenario of great power war on the other. Of course, realistic global scenarios are not entirely positive or negative ones, short of truly extreme catastrophes, and feature a variable mix of desirable and undesirable developments. The question is, however, what trends prevail, and with what consequences. The trends and drivers outlined in this book point to considerable chances of further deterioration of global politics, economics and security. In other words, a regressive world, while far from predetermined, appears a realistic baseline scenario if there is not strong engagement to avert it.

Taking a broad perspective, the emerging picture is one of reversal of the achievements of the last three decades, since the end of the Cold War. This reversal is not a sudden twist. Evidence of it has been piling up over the last ten or fifteen years – for example, the financial crisis and its manifold consequences, the rise of populism, the return of Russia's imperialism, China's increasingly assertive and antagonistic posture, the nationalist turn in the US under Trump, and rising tensions among superpowers. Since 2020, however, the Covid pandemic and Russia's attack on Ukraine have precipitated the drift from a world of relative progress, despite tensions and setbacks, to one of regression.

To be sure, regression may look different if assessed in Brussels, Washington, Beijing, Dubai, Delhi, Ankara, Pretoria or Brasilia. Growth patterns have widely diverged, power has been shifting and, more broadly, what is a crisis for one can be an opportunity for another. The case should be made, however, that the picture needs widening. The focus here is not on the relative rise of some or the relative decline of others, as important as that is, but on the degradation of the political, strategic, economic and ecological stage on which all the powers play. On practical grounds, this trend threatens their interests and those of humanity at large, since it undermines geopolitical stability, economic exchanges and human security. At the normative level, values long-regarded as universal, such as those enshrined in the UN Charter and the Universal Declaration of Human Rights, are increasingly contested. Manifestations and drivers of a regressive world abound.

Development and human security have clearly reversed. More people are hungry, displaced or otherwise at risk today than five years ago and several factors point to this challenge exacerbating. Since the start of the pandemic in particular, progress on women's rights has been rolled back and vulnerable groups and individuals face more challenges. While conflict statistics are subject to abrupt variations, the number of both state-based and nonstate conflicts has been steadily on the rise for over ten years. In 2022 the number of battle-related deaths was the highest since 1984.[34] With geopolitical tensions mounting, global military expenditure has been growing for many years[35] and can be expected to keep rising, which will likely put pressure on other spending priorities.

---

34   Obermeier, A. M., and Rustad S. A. (2023) "Conflict trends: a global overview, 1946–2022". PRIO Paper, Peace Research Institute Oslo.
35   SIPRI (2023) *SIPRI Yearbook 2023: Armaments, Disarmament and International Security* (Oxford University Press) (https://www.sipri.org/yearbook/2023).

In advanced economies, successive economic crises, policies favouring capital over labour and the impact of new technologies on jobs have depressed the real income of average households, spurring the so-called crisis of the middle class that has fuelled populist politics. While growth prospects of course differ from region to region, the global economic outlook is rather grim, as the world faces a combination of supply shocks (from the pandemic to the war in Ukraine and the many potential implications of geoeconomic competition) and consequent high inflation. The latter pushes interest rates up and compounds stress on public and private debt, whose size relative to GDP has massively grown in recent years and continues expanding. Leaving aside the risk that new major disruptions blow up this precarious balance, great power competition will at any rate depress growth prospects relative to a cooperative scenario of open (if managed) flows.

Geopolitics trumping economics and multilateralism means a world sleepwalking over steep downward slopes, leading to multiple potential cliffs. On some level, interdependence can be chosen, for example, by opening or closing trade and investment flows. On another level, interdependence is simply systemic and factual, as in the obvious cases of climate change and pandemics. The costs of not adequately addressing these and other common challenges have been massive in recent years and are projected to skyrocket, notably because of the impact of climate change. With major powers increasingly absorbed by competition and short-term calculations, there is a clear risk of a leaderless world at a time when collective action would be of the essence. This also applies to the wide-ranging implications of technological innovation, from artificial intelligence to quantum computing, which is becoming a new arena of weaponised connectivity and incremental decoupling.

Among other levels of competition, the normative dimension reflects and harbours more potential for regression. Pretty much all the indicators pertaining to democracy and human rights have been deteriorating in the last decade. To take but one example, the share of the world population living in (closed or electoral) autocracies jumped from 46% in 2012 to 72% in 2022.[36] The surge of revisionist and authoritarian powers such as China and Russia has compounded this trend and sets a systemic challenge to democracy and the rule of law worldwide, including via political interference in liberal democracies.[37] Meanwhile, populist and nationalist

---

36 V-Dem Institute (2023) "Democracy report 2023: defiance in the face of autocratization". University of Gothenburg, March.
37 See Chapter 1, by Korniychuk.

political forces have planted deep roots in democratic countries. While there is evidence of both the rise and fall, or the expansion and containment, of populist waves in the democratic world, far-right parties and narratives have become a more important factor in domestic politics than they were one or two decades ago, and the drivers of discontent that have in part fuelled them have not abated.

Counterarguments could of course be deployed to challenge this scenario of regression.[38] These include the growing levels of human security and development seen up until recently; the potential of technological innovation to improve the environment, global health, education and welfare at large; fast-rising investment in renewable energy; the structural weaknesses of authoritarian regimes; the capacity of democracies to adapt and bounce back in the face of crises; the mitigating effects of economic interdependence on geopolitical competition; and the overall resilience of globalisation so far.

It should be reiterated that no future is preordained. But two points need stressing. First, the factors and forces of regression are stronger now than at any stage since the end of the Cold War. Second, the prospect of a regressive world, however daunting, is not a worst-case scenario. For example, it does not contemplate the potential escalation of the war in Ukraine, or the disruptive impact of China attacking Taiwan. The regressive world is in fact a business-as-usual scenario. It draws on the trends that have emerged and intensified over the last decade or so and that Russia's war in Ukraine, coming on the heels of the Covid pandemic, has taken to a potential tipping point. In fact, if further developed and nuanced, this scenario could be a useful basis for a backcasting exercise. In foresight, backcasting consists of delineating a desirable or undesirable scenario and then working backwards to establish how to attain, or avoid, it. Being clear-eyed about the prospect of a regressive world is the essential first step to express the political leadership and strategic vision required to prevent it from materialising and to steer the world in a better direction.

The European Union: deepening or faltering?

Whether the prospect of a regressive world will fully materialise depends not only on structural trends or the impact of disruptive events but also

---

38   For a set of arguments and data pointing to relative progress on many fronts (before the pandemic and the war in Ukraine), see, for example, Pinker, S. (2018) *Enlightenment Now: The Case for Reason, Science, Humanism and Progress* (New York: Penguin, Viking).

on the political choices, priorities and strategies of pivotal state and non-state actors. The EU is certainly one of the actors that can help make a difference. However, the upheaval of Europe's global strategic context, which Russia's war in Ukraine is both a symptom and a major driver of, will put the EU to a truly unprecedented test in the coming 5–10 years. How the EU will stand this test will be decisive to its leadership in helping steer Europe and the world away from regression.

For the past 15 years at least, the EU has coped with cascading crises that fuelled each other and strained its political, economic and social cohesion. The common denominator to most of them, from the financial crisis to the destabilisation of the EU's neighbourhood and the election of Trump in 2016, is that they originated from abroad. To a large extent, therefore, convergence or divergence among EU member states during this extended polycrisis has been the product of the interplay between external trends, or shocks, and domestic politics.[39]

Up until the Covid pandemic hit Europe in early 2020, member states had laboriously managed to patch together partial or technical solutions to successive crises. While effective at containing them, these measures did not address underlying political problems, whether the lack of an EU fiscal capacity, of a credible common asylum policy or of a viable defence policy. As compromises were struck on different measures, EU politics grew more polarised, within and between countries. The impacts of the pandemic and of Russia's full-scale invasion of Ukraine have marked a step change, sparking EU member states to take joint responsibility and commit to momentous decisions in the face of existential challenges. They recognised that working through the EU (and NATO) was imperative to deliver effective action on an adequate scale.

The question is whether this approach will last over the next decade. As highlighted in this book, the Union faces a growing range of short- and long-term security, economic, political and normative challenges at once. Many of those are not new, but most of them are worsening and will require a degree of mobilisation and convergence among EU countries and institutions that greatly surpasses the progress made so far. Looking at current and envisaged developments on the international stage, three important differences with the past EU track record of crisis management need stressing. These concern the conception of the EU as a power, the resilience of the Union, and its very shape and architecture.

---

[39] Grevi, G. (forthcoming) "Convergence and divergence in EU foreign and security policy", in Telò, M. (ed.) *Towards a Common EU Strategic Culture?* (Brussels: Académie Royale de Belgique).

First, just as economic, political and security challenges are ever more intimately interconnected, the distinction between different dimensions of EU power in the world needs revising. In a contested world of power politics, being a geopolitical power is not necessarily an alternative, or impediment, to performing as a normative or regulatory one, but arguably a condition for that role. Strength matters even when pursuing inclusive dialogues about rules and norms to address shared challenges. Likewise, norms, rules and support for effective multilateralism are critical dimensions of power, hard and soft, since competition takes place across all of these dimensions at once. Of course, tensions and trade-offs will continue to exist between these different dimensions of EU power, but they will need to be faced and managed, not ignored or denied.

Second, developments on the home front will be decisive in enhancing or diminishing the EU's clout and influence abroad. This is of course not a new finding, but both old and new vulnerabilities will require much more political and economic investment to preserve Europe's cohesion. Higher energy prices and a global subsidies race are affecting the competitiveness of European industry, while inflation and sluggish growth threaten the living standards of a growing share of society. State intervention to offset the impact of these factors risks unbalancing the single market and placing excessive burdens on national public debts.[40] The single market (and the euro) give the EU strategic depth in geoeconomic competition, which makes completing the services market and the capital union critically important steps to enable growth and larger volumes of investment in European companies.

Scaling up public and private investment will similarly be decisive to sustain the green and digital transitions, improving Europe's innovation potential and reducing the EU's dependence on the technology of others.[41] This will in turn provide the long-term bedrock of Europe's famed regulatory power. Another key risk for Europe's resilience would be the green and digital transitions turning from sources of competitiveness and international leadership to sources of social stress and political divisions in Europe. For both transitions, much has been achieved, but the hard part is yet to come, whether considering the job market or costs for households. The impact of automation on jobs will depend in part on providing the workforce with adequate skills and pathways to shift to new occupations. There is evidence that the consensus on the green transition is fissuring

---

40 See Chapter 7, by Schwarzer.
41 On prospects for the energy transition in Europe, see Chapter 3, by Pellerin-Carlin.

as the price of it becomes more tangible for families and companies. The twin transitions losing steam would impair both Europe's long-term growth and the soft power of the EU. But these ambitious transitions will not meet their goals if they will not be fair ones too, in terms of their economic and social implications.[42] Revamping the European social contract to match the needs of the emerging technological revolution would additionally make politics and society more resilient to interference and hybrid tactics by Russia, China and others, ready to leverage discontent in order to weaken Europe's unity and geopolitical resolve.

Third, Russia's aggression of Ukraine has been a watershed moment for Europe's political and security order. The war has reframed and revived the tired debate on EU enlargement to Eastern Europe and the Western Balkans and triggered unprecedented steps, with Ukraine, Moldova and Bosnia Herzegovina achieving EU candidate status in 2022. The prospect for the EU to expand to up to 35 members, if conditions are fulfilled, has opened up. But the road to get there is long and the pace of progress will depend on critical political questions that are yet to be fully addressed. Aside from the obvious need for far-reaching structural and political reforms in candidate countries, this is a paradigm shift for the EU itself, in both policy and institutional terms.[43] A few small countries could perhaps be absorbed with relatively minor tweaks to EU policies, competences and decision-making rules. However, there is little chance of the EU enlarging to eight new countries, including a large one like Ukraine, without a significant reform of its budget, redistributive policies (namely, agriculture and cohesion) and institutional framework.

There are very strong strategic, political and economic arguments backing the new drive to expand the EU and lock in peace, democracy and prosperity across the continent. But in the years to come the enlargement will take place in a far less benign international context than that of the 1990s and 2000s – one that will require EU member states to pool resources and sovereignty to a much greater extent than in the past. As argued above, the EU needs to be stronger at home to carry weight abroad and cope with multidimensional competition. This is why large-scale EU enlargement without deepening would weaken the Union. The alternative

---

42   On the connections between social and economic issues, sustainability, and the EU's external projection, see European Commission (2023) "2023 Strategic Foresight Report: sustainability and people's wellbeing at the heart of Europe's Open Strategic Autonomy". COM(2023) 376, July (https://commission.europa.eu/document/download/f8f67d33-194c-4c89-a4a6-795980a1dabd_en?filename=SFR-23_en.pdf).

43   See Chapter 7, by Schwarzer.

is no longer the much-debated old dilemma between deepening and enlarging. Today and in coming years, the real alternative is between deepening and faltering. The prospect of enlargement should be one of the strongest drivers of progress to deepen and empower the EU.

From firefighting to forest management

This book has found that the geopolitical paradigm is expected to continue to permeate international affairs, shape political debates and inform strategic choices for the foreseeable future. The prevalence of the geopolitical perspective also heightens the risk of tensions and instability sparking further conflicts, including among great powers, which was until recently considered a remote possibility. If a geopolitical mindset has taken hold in many capitals, however, economic interdependence has so far proved quite resilient, and transnational challenges threaten to inflict severe costs on humanity. Recognising that geopolitics is a central dimension of international relations does not mean accepting that it is, or should be, the only paradigm framing strategic challenges and choices ahead. That would be a very narrow, short-term approach.

There is a clear risk that Russia's war in Ukraine contributes to exacerbating and eventually locking in many of the negative trends that have emerged in earlier years, tilting the balance from an already contested and competitive world to one of systemic rivalry and regression. This is not an inevitable prospect, but one that will take strong leadership to ward off. For the EU to play a leading role in this effort, as it can and should do, Europeans need to heed three basic lessons that Russia's aggression has forcefully pressed home.

The first lesson is a short and sobering one: hope is not a strategy. To put it differently, many of the challenges that look bad today are likely to get worse, if not adequately addressed. This is not a recipe for surrender, but an antidote to inaction and to a subtler form of resignation: determinism.

The second lesson is that damage limitation is not enough to inform long-term leadership. In other words, firefighting, while necessary, is no substitute for forest management. This applies just as well to the management of global economic interdependence, to the fight against climate change, to the pursuit of sustainable development, to grasping and governing the implications of unprecedented technological innovation, to defence strategies, and to far-sighted diplomacy.

To be sure, firefighting (quick responses or ad hoc measures) is essential to cope with shocks or crises. The rather effective transatlantic reaction to Russia's aggression against Ukraine is a clear case in point. There is a problem, however, if firefighting becomes endemic and blurs or detracts from forest management (comprehensive, long-term approaches to tackle systemic challenges). Examples abound. The dramatic mismanagement of migrant and refugee flows is a stark example of emergency measures devoid of a viable strategy. While driven by a sound assessment of the underlying problem, piecemeal progress on the global stage to mitigate and adapt to climate change falls short of what is required to contain the rise of global temperatures under sustainable levels.

In the case of the EU, the difference between firefighting and forest management can be applied to various topical issues on the agenda of the next decade. Concerning geoeconomics, for example, the emerging economic security agenda – focused on derisking economic interdependence with China and other competitors or rivals, and on responding to economic coercion – is a necessary component of economic statecraft in a world of power politics. However, taken on its own, it is closer to firefighting than to forest management. The latter entails completing the single market, the capital union and the banking union, and endowing the EU with a permanent, adequate fiscal capacity, as part of a broader revision of the EU's fiscal framework.[44] These reforms would also enable much larger public and private investments in order to sustain Europe's green and digital transitions and preserve social and political support for them. This is all the more important considering that the NextGenerationEU instrument (a good initial effort at forest management) will expire in 2026.

In defence matters, some useful steps have been taken to foster cooperation among EU member states on capability development and procurement, the European Peace Facility has been quickly mobilised to support Ukraine, and national governments have launched uncoordinated but relatively sizeable defence spending programmes to start offsetting decades of underinvestment. Moving from firefighting to forest management would require, for example, achieving much closer coordination of national defence planning processes, building a stronger technological

---

44   On the need to redefine the EU's fiscal framework to face challenges ahead and enhance Europe's capacity to act, see Draghi, M. (2023) "The next flight of the bumblebee: the path to a common fiscal policy in the eurozone". Fifteenth Annual Feldstein Lecture, National Bureau of Economic Research, 11 July.

and industrial base for European defence, and integrating European military forces into large units, which would both contribute to Europe's defence within NATO and be able to operate on their own if needed.[45]

One of the biggest forest management challenges that awaits the EU over the next decade is the redesign of the European political and security order following Russia's war in Ukraine. The EU's enlargement to the Western Balkans and Eastern Europe will be a pivotal dimension of this undertaking. Facing the challenges and opportunities of EU enlargement with a firefighting mentality would be a grave strategic mistake for the Union. This is not about ignoring the difficult politics, and geopolitics, of the enlargement process, neglecting the several conditions that candidate countries must fulfil, or bypassing the requirement to reform EU policies and institutions to ensure that a larger Union works well. It is about tackling the many challenges that will undoubtedly emerge on the long road to enlargement with a clear sense of the end goal. Enlargement should be one of the key engines of EU reform, as opposed to (lack of) EU reform becoming an obstacle to enlargement, which would cripple the credibility of the EU as an international actor.

This book has shown that strengthening Europe's unity, security and prosperity is important not only to withstand competition in a world of power politics but also to empower the EU's leadership and help avert the scenario of a regressive world. The third lessons for Europeans is that this higher strategic goal, while a defining one for the EU, should be handled with care. The only way to bring about the sort of rules-based world order that Europeans aspire to is to start from the world as it is, which is not a pretty place. That said, recognising this reality and acting consequently (for example, by strengthening the EU as a full-fledged geopolitical power and beating back Russia's invasion of Ukraine) is not tantamount to simply accepting the world as it is, and playing by the rules of power while the international order unravels.

The EU must indeed learn "the language of power", and it has made some significant progress on that score. But while learning this language, it should also use it to have thorough conversations about progress, justice, cooperation, shared challenges and opportunities. As it has been put recently, the EU cannot be multilateral on its own.[46] It is also clear

---

45 See Chapter 1, by Korniychuk.

46 European Commission and High Representative of the Union for Foreign Affairs and Security Policy (2021) "Joint Communication to the European Parliament and the Council on strengthening the EU's contribution to rules-based multilateralism". JOIN(2021) 3 final, 17 February.

that frameworks for cooperation will need to be flexible, depending on the scope for cooperation with different sets of actors on different matters. At the same time, there is little chance of a rules-based global order surviving without the EU pressing forward and engaging others to repel aggression (in Ukraine and elsewhere), preserve a reasonably open international economic order and deliver desperately needed global public goods. The EU's geopolitical, normative and regulatory power will need to be much more closely connected to ward off a regressive world.

About the authors

ELVIRE FABRY

Elvire Fabry is senior research fellow in charge of geopolitics of trade at the Jacques Delors Institute and rapporteur of the EU–China working group. She is a member of the board of the Centre d'Etudes Prospectives et d'Informations Internationales, a leading French centre for research and expertise on the world economy; of the Policy Advisory Committee of the German Marshall Fund of the United States in Paris; of the Scientific Council of the Elcano Royal Institute; of the board of Futuribles International; of the editorial board of the foresight journal *Futuribles*; and of the Jean Monnet Network on Transatlantic Trade Politics. She holds a PhD in political science (Sciences Po, Paris). She was an auditor of the 64th session on defence policy of the Institute of Higher National Defence Studies (2011–2012).

GIOVANNI GREVI

Giovanni Grevi is a senior fellow at the Centre for Security, Diplomacy and Strategy of the Brussels School of Governance (BSoG-VUB). He teaches European foreign policy and international relations at the BSoG-VUB; at the College of Europe, Bruges; and at Sciences Po, Paris. Giovanni has worked and published extensively on EU foreign and security policy, global order, foresight, US foreign policy, and EU politics and institutions. Between 2016 and 2020 Giovanni was head of the Europe in the World programme and senior fellow at the European Policy Centre (EPC). Previously, he worked at the Foundation for International Relations and External Dialogue (FRIDE) as director and senior researcher (2010–2015). Giovanni served as a senior research fellow at the EU Institute for Security Studies from 2005 to 2010 and worked at the EPC as policy analyst and associate director of studies (1999–2005). He is a senior associate fellow with the Italian Institute for International Political Studies (ISPI) and the EPC. Giovanni holds a PhD from the Université Libre de Bruxelles and an MSc from the London School of Economics.

ANDRIY KORNIYCHUK

Andriy Korniychuk is a policy analyst at the Foundation for European Progressive Studies. Before joining its Brussels office he cooperated with FEPS in the capacity of a nonresident postdoctoral fellow, focusing on the EU's enlargement and neighbourhood policies, with particular attention to Ukraine's postwar recovery and its EU accession path. Prior to that, Andriy worked as the head of the Europe and International Affairs and Baltic Dialogue programmes at the Warsaw office of the Heinrich Böll Foundation and was responsible for the Eastern Europe and Eurasia programme at the largest peacebuilding organization in the Netherlands (PAX). Previously, he also worked on migration management within the UN system (the International Organization for Migration and the United Nations High Commissioner for Refugees). Andriy is a member of the European Studies Unit at the Institute of Sociology and Philosophy of the Polish Academy of Sciences, where he successfully defended a doctoral dissertation entitled "Democratic legitimacy beyond a nation-state: the case of the European Union". He is an alumnus of Maastricht University (MA in European public affairs) and Lancaster University (MA in politics and society). His research interests include the analysis of the ongoing transformational processes in the EU and its neighbourhood, and their international context. Andriy has contributed to over 40 publications and has provided expert input for media outlets in Europe and the US.

GEORGE PAPACONSTANTINOU

George Papaconstantinou is professor of international political economy at the School of Transnational Governance of the European University Institute (EUI) and the EUI Dean for Executive Education. He studied economics in the UK and the US, obtaining a PhD in the subject from the London School of Economics. He worked for ten years at the Organisation for Economic Co-operation and Development in Paris. After being elected to the Greek parliament and the European Parliament, in 2009 he was appointed finance minister and from that position played a key role in the Greek crisis, negotiating the first Greek bailout. Subsequently, as Minister of Environment and Energy, he pursued policies to advance Greece's sustainable growth agenda. His book on the crisis, *Game Over: The Inside Story of the Greek Crisis*, has been published in Greek, English and German. His recently published book *Whatever It Takes: The Battle for Post-crisis Europe* debates the lessons from the eurozone crisis for EU governance in the context of current challenges. His current research focuses on the economics and politics of crises, the political economy of European integration and the transformation of global governance.

THOMAS PELLERIN-CARLIN

Thomas Pellerin-Carlin is the director of the European programme at the Institute for Climate Economics (I4CE), which he joined in 2022. He also teaches at Sciences Po in Paris and at the Energy Union training programme of the College of Europe in Bruges. Before joining the I4CE, Thomas worked at the Jacques Delors Institute, where he started in 2015 as an EU energy policy research fellow before founding and directing the Jacques Delors Energy Centre (2018–2022). He also worked for the College of Europe in Belgium (2013–2015) as academic assistant and research assistant of its European Energy Policy Chair. Previously, he worked for the French administration (General Secretariat for European Affairs, 2012) and the French army and its Defence Staff. Thomas studied political science and holds an MA from the College of Europe's Master in European Political and Administrative Studies programme (2012–2013, Václav Havel Promotion) and an MA from Sciences Po Lille (2007–2012, Promotion George Orwell).

ANNALISA PRIZZON

Annalisa Prizzon is principal research fellow at the global affairs think tank ODI. She has more than 15 years of experience researching and advising governments and multilateral agencies on policies for the allocation, effectiveness and architecture of international public finance. She worked in several countries in sub-Saharan Africa, Southeast Asia, the Pacific and Latin America. Before joining the ODI, Annalisa was an economist and policy analyst in academic institutions and international organisations (the Organisation for Economic Co-operation and Development and the World Bank Group). She holds a PhD in economics and public finance, with a focus on external debt sustainability in low-income countries. Annalisa is a Council member of the Development Studies Association, lead editor of *Development Policy Review* and member of the Committee for Development Policy for the 2022–2024 term. She also served as a member of the World Economic Forum Global Future Council on Infrastructure in 2019 and 2020.

DANIELA SCHWARZER

Prof. Dr Daniela Schwarzer is a member of the Bertelsmann Stiftung's Executive Board and honorary professor of political science at Freie Universität Berlin. She is a leading expert on European and international affairs and has had a 20-year career at renowned think tanks, foundations and universities. From 2021 to 2023, she served as executive director for Europe and Central Asia at the Open Society Foundations, the world's largest foundation working to strengthen the rule of law, democracy and open societies. In autumn 2022, she was a visiting professor at Harvard University, with which she has also been affiliated as a senior fellow. From 2016 to 2021, Daniela directed the German Council on Foreign Relations. Prior to that, she served as research director on the executive team of the German Marshall Fund of the United States and led its Berlin office and Europe programme. From 2004 to 2013, she worked for the German Institute for International and Security Affairs and beginning in 2008 headed its Europe research group. From 1999 to 2004, she was an opinion page editor and France correspondent for the *Financial Times Deutschland*.

THIJS VAN DE GRAAF

Thijs Van de Graaf is an associate professor of international politics at Ghent University, where he is the co-coordinator of the Ghent Institute for International and European Studies. He is also a nonresident fellow with Johns Hopkins University, the Colorado School of Mines and the United Nations University. In 2011 he was a visiting researcher at Princeton University. Thijs specializes in global energy politics, particularly in the oil and gas markets, climate policy, hydrogen, critical materials, and the geopolitical effects of the energy transition. His latest book, *Global Energy Politics*, was published in 2020 with Polity Press. He was also the lead author of three reports on the geopolitics of the energy transition for the International Renewable Energy Agency. His research has been cited in media such as *The Guardian*, *The Independent* and the *Washington Post*.